D1562067

Dimensions of Ethnicity

A Series of Selections from the
Harvard Encyclopedia of American Ethnic Groups

Stephan Thernstrom, *Editor*
Ann Orlov, *Managing Editor*
Oscar Handlin, *Consulting Editor*

THE AMERICAN JEWS

ARTHUR A. GOREN

*The Belknap Press of
Harvard University Press
Cambridge, Massachusetts
London, England
1982*

Library of Congress Cataloging in Publication Data

Goren, Arthur A., 1926–
    The American Jews.

    (Dimensions of ethnicity)
    Originally published in: Harvard encyclopedia of American ethnic groups.
1980.
    Bibliography: p.
    1. Jews—United States—History.   2. United States—Emigration and
immigration—History.   3. United States—Ethnic
relations.   I. Title.   II. Series.
E184.J5G6743   1982   305.8'924'073   82-11699
ISBN 0-674-02516-4 (pbk.)

Foreword

Ethnicity is a central theme—perhaps the central theme—of American history. From the first encounters between Englishmen and Indians at Jamestown down to today's "boat people," the interplay between peoples of differing national origins, religions, and races has shaped the character of our national life. Although scholars have long recognized this fact, in the past two decades they have paid it more heed than ever before. The result has been an explosive increase in research on America's complex ethnic mosaic. Examination of a recent bibliography of doctoral dissertations on ethnic themes written between 1899 and 1972 reveals that no less than half of them appeared in the years 1962–1972. The pace of inquiry has not slackened since then; it has accelerated.

The extraordinary proliferation of literature on ethnicity and ethnic groups made possible—and necessary—an effort to take stock. An authoritative, up-to-date synthesis of the current state of knowledge in the field was called for. The *Harvard Encyclopedia of American Ethnic Groups,* published by the Harvard University Press in 1980, is such a synthesis. It provides entries by leading scholars on the origins, history, and present situation of the more than 100 ethnic groups that make up the population of the United States, and 29 thematic essays on a wide range of ethnic topics. As one reviewer said, the volume is "a kind of *summa ethnica* of our time."

I am pleased that some of the most interesting and valuable articles in the encyclopedia are now available to a wider audience through inexpenisve paperback editions such as this one. These essays will be an excellent starting point for anyone in search of deeper understanding of who the American people are and how they came to be that way.

Stephan Thernstrom

Contents

The American Jews

Since 1654, when the first group of 23 Jews arrived in New Amsterdam, Jewish migration to the United States has been nearly continuous. Meager during the colonial and early national periods, it increased substantially in the middle third of the 19th century; by 1880 approximately 180,000 Jews had come to the United States. From 2,000 in 1790, the estimated Jewish population rose to 6,000 by 1830, to 150,000 by 1860, and to 250,000 by 1880. Then the number soared. Beginning in 1882 and continuing for the next 42 years, some 2.3 million Jews entered the country. By 1924 the Jewish population stood at 4.2 million. The restrictive quotas that went into effect in 1924 reduced the immigration precipitously, and the Depression lowered it still further. It rose again just before and after World War II. Between 1925 and 1975 576,000 Jews entered the United States. In 1977 the Jewish population was an estimated 5.4 million (see Table 1).

The ebb and flow of immigration constituted one element in the social and ethnic configuration of the American Jewish population; its diverse origins constituted another. The successive migrations came from countries with disparate cultures and political systems, different social and economic conditions, separate poli-

**Table 1. Jewish Population in the United States,
1790–1980**

Year	Number	Percentage of total population
1790	1,500	0.05
1830	6,000	.05
1860	150,000	.47
1880	250,000	.50
1888	400,000	.66
1900	1,058,000	1.39
1920	3,390,000	3.18
1940	4,770,000	3.61
1960	5,367,000	2.99
1980	5,500,000[a]	2.42

Source: *American Jewish Yearbook*, 77(1977): 252, 257–
262, 267–273, 290–292; 81(1981): 165.
a. Does not include non-Jewish members of Jewish
households; 400,000 non-Jews are estimated to be members
of Jewish households.

cies regarding their Jewish minority, and variant ethnic traditions.

Language was one index of this diversity. Spanish-
and Portuguese-speaking Jews (Sephardim), with roots
in the Iberian Peninsula, established the earliest Jewish
settlements in the New World. They were joined by
Jews from the German-speaking areas of central Europe
and from Poland (Ashkenazim) who spoke Yiddish, a
language derived from Middle High German, with elements of Hebrew, Aramaic and whatever the language
of the host culture happened to be. The mid-19th-cen-
tury immigrants from Bavaria and Prussian Posen (now
Polish Poznań) spoke Western Yiddish, Polish Yiddish, or, in the case of the more acculturated, German.

Jews from Lithuania, Poland, the Ukraine, Galicia, Hungary, and Romania, who came in the great migration from eastern Europe beginning in the 1880s, were distinguishable by their regional Yiddish dialects. Jews arriving from the disintegrating Ottoman Empire in the early 1900s, from Nazi Germany before World War II, and from Europe, Latin America, and Israel after it spoke Ladino, Arabic, German, Yiddish, Hungarian, Spanish, Hebrew, and Russian.

Different times of arrival accentuated the disparities. The social and economic conditions prevailing in the United States at the time of entry largely determined the pattern of individual integration and influenced the evolving ethnic community. The arrival of the Jews spanned the colonial settlement, western expansion, and industrial and urban growth, changing conditions that corresponded in some degree with the changing origins of the immigrants. German Jews, who predominated in the years before the Civil War, spread out across the continent and filled mercantile roles in an expanding economy. They acculturated rapidly and moved into the middle class with relative ease. Eastern European Jews, arriving a half-century or more later, joined the industrial labor force or became suppliers of consumer goods and services in the immigrant neighborhoods. The intense ethnic life in these enclaves underscored the cultural and class differences between the Americanized Jews and the newcomers.

The size and vitality of the large immigrant communities also intensified the divisions induced by old-country localism and religious-secular antagonisms,

competing ideological movements, and conflicting ap-
proaches to communal needs. The refugees of the 1930s
and 1940s, though far fewer, added a heterogeneous
new stratum to the Jewish population. Those from Germany were largely middle-class professionals with
deep roots in European culture. They had little in common with the ultra-Orthodox Jews arriving about the
same time, who were bent on establishing closed sectarian communities. The German refugees had little
rapport with the descendants of the earlier German immigration, and the ultra-Orthodox did not mix with the
Americanized Orthodox Jewish community.

THE ETHNIC HERITAGE
AND THE EUROPEAN EXPERIENCE

Although the diversity of cultural and social back-
grounds strained the ties of community, the counter-
vailing force of a venerable heritage imposed a sense of
group identity. Jews perceived their ethnic existence as
part of an historic and religious continuum that extended back to Biblical times. Scripture not only con-
veyed the ritual and ethical teachings of Judaism but
celebrated the origins of the nation, which was elaborated in the post-Biblical tradition of a people in exile
awaiting redemption. The fusion of a universal faith
with belief in national restoration found expression in
a messianism that saw Israel as God's instrument for
bringing salvation to the world. For the Jews, survival
was a sacred obligation.

This notion of a consecrated people manifested itself in an exacting religious culture that permeated Jewish life until challenged by modern, secular influences. Although there were periods of fruitful interchange between Jews and non-Jews (in Spain from the 10th to 14th centuries), externally imposed and self-imposed barriers persisted. Increasing governmental repression, which reached a high point in the walled ghettos and expulsions of the late Middle Ages, turned the Jews inward and intensified their separatism, especially among the Ashkenazi Jews whose settlements, first in France and Germany and later in eastern Europe, became the centers of an austere but vigorous rabbinical Judaism. Revered rabbinical scholars, the interpreters and teachers of the tradition, exercised a decisive influence through their academies and as communal leaders. Religious study was required of every male child, urged upon every male adult, and rewarded by status in society. Scripture, ritual, Talmudic law (*halacha*), and customs, summarized in codes and homiletic tracts, regulated the moral, religious, and cultural life of the Jews.

A Jewish polity—the *kehillah*—provided the framework for group life. The halacha recognized the right of each Jewish settlement to form its own kehillah and adopt its own self-governing regulations. Secular rulers, for reasons of convenience, custom, and profit, treated the Jews as a corporate group accountable for the acts and obligations of its members. The Jewish community received a measure of autonomy in taxation, civil law, and administration, powers that the kehillah leadership, both lay and rabbinical, used to reinforce their authority over the private and public life of the Jews. In this way the community achieved the cohesion and discipline needed to face an alien and threatening society.

Christendom's hostility toward the Jews had been fed by inverting the Jewish notion that they were a people set apart; instead of an elect group, the Christians considered them pariahs. Stigmatized as "Christ killers," Jews lived a precarious existence beyond the pale of the social order and depended upon the uncertain protection of ruler or monarch. Prohibited from owning land or employing Gentiles and forced out of manufacture and handicrafts by the craft guilds, Jews gravitated to occupations that Christians considered risky, demeaning, or sinful. Their concentration in commerce, especially money-lending and tax-collecting, exposed them to exploitation by their protectors and to the fury of impoverished peasants and insolvent noblemen. This endemic antipathy erupted periodically in epidemics of violence. The First Crusade in 1096 set the pattern of pillage and massacre. In the Rhine Valley, a center of Jewish life, whole communities were destroyed, and secular and ecclesiastical authorities were powerless to contain the mobs. Contemporary Jewish and Gentile accounts recorded the acts of martyrdom of Jews who refused baptism and were slain. Martyrdom—"the sanctification of the Name [of God]"—became a dominant theme in the homiletic and pietistic literature of Ashkenazi Jewry.

The idea of the Jew as demon entered the folklore

and literature of Europe and deepened the chasm separating Jews from Gentiles. Images of the Jew as sorcerer and "the devil incarnate" who mutilated the Host and used Christian blood for ritual purposes led to trials, executions, and expulsions; at the end of the 13th century, Jews were driven from England en masse, and at the end of the 14th century from France.

In 1492 the most massive expulsion took place in Spain, where the Jews were forced to choose between exile and conversion. Nearly 150,000 Jews left Spain, and about 50,000 converted, bringing to an end a communal history of 700 years. Most of them established themselves in the Muslim countries bordering the Mediterranean.

Ashkenazi Jews were moving eastward into Poland at about the same time, attracted by a relatively benign regime that needed their skills. They dominated the export-import trade, leased royal lands, and served as tax farmers; the great majority were tradesmen, artisans, or lessees of mills, distilleries, and similar occupations. By 1600 about 500,000 Jews were living in eastern Europe, perhaps twice as many as remained in the isolated Jewish pockets of central and western Europe. The Polish settlement was the heartland of European Jewry, its religious and cultural center.

Polish Jewry created a network of regional and national councils and courts that acted as a minority self-government. On the local level the kehillah combined a strong council of elected elders drawn from the wealthy and learned and a wide-ranging network of voluntary associations. The council oversaw the communal government, assisted in the larger communities by paid officials: the town rabbi, rabbinical judges, an emissary to the Gentile authorities, teachers, administrators, clerks, and inspectors. The various voluntary associations interred the dead, ministered to the sick, cared for orphans, provided for paupers and wayfarers, maintained the free school for needy children, studied the Bible or Talmud, and performed similar functions. Artisans established guilds, and the synagogues had supporting societies. Social and religious activities were integral to these societies, and many provided welfare benefits for their members. In all, community life involved many of the residents and gave them considerable experience in communal government.

In the mid-17th century, eastern European Jewry entered a long, dark age of tribulation. Government oppression pauperized the group, and political convulsions such as the uprising of the Ukrainian Cossacks under Bogdan Chmielnicki in 1648 threatened its survival. In the anarchy that marked the disintegration of the Polish state in the 18th century, the Jews were decimated; many fled, and those who remained led a perilous existence that weakened community life. Hasidism, a pietistic religious revival and a disruptive force of another kind, found favor among the humbler folk because of its emphasis on spontaneity rather than knowledge, and on the role of charismatic leaders, or *zaddikim*. In time, these religious and social antagonisms abated, but they left behind bitter memories of schisms, which were later carried to the United States.

In the 19th century eastern European Jewry was divided among Prussia (the Posen region), Austria (the much larger Galician community), and Russia (most of Polish Jewry). The governments of all three viewed the Jews as an alien and backward element that ultimately was to be absorbed by the native population. The implementation of this goal varied from the relatively mild and partly successful tactics of Prussia to the enlightened despotism of the Hapsburgs and the draconian methods of tsarist Russia, which, aside from a brief interlude in the 1860s, maintained a systematic policy of oppression. The imperial ukase of 1827, for example, extended conscription to the Jews, with the proviso that their service last for 25 years. When quotas were not filled, children as young as 12 were conscripted or abducted. Conversion was the goal of Russian policy. Jewish folk songs, memoirs, and literature reflect the loneliness, brutal treatment, and martyrdom of those who were snatched away and the terror and despair of all Russia's Jews. Expulsion from the villages and exorbitant taxes were other methods used to reform the Jews; in 1844 the tsar abolished kehillah self-government, which it considered an obstacle to assimilation.

In western Europe, the Enlightenment and the French Revolution altered the status of the Jews. Secular modes of thought opened the way for the emergence of a religiously neutral society. In the enlightened circles where a rationalist approach to religion, society, economics, and politics was current, Jews of similar persuasion found acceptance. Jewish emancipation, granted first by France in 1790, came slowly and uncertainly to the rest of western Europe: Prussia (1850), England (1858), and Austria-Hungary (1867). Even in the classic instance of France, citizenship was granted on condition that the Jews renounce the notion of Jewish nationality, discard their separate laws, and dissolve their self-governing institutions. Among the new nation-states, the prevailing assumption was that emancipation would bring assimilation.

The secularly educated, upper-class stratum of western Jewry responded with alacrity to the opportunity to be rid of the ancient disabilities and restrictions imposed by both the Gentile and traditional Jewish societies. Some embraced Christianity, others sought to retain their Jewish identity in ways that would not hinder their social and cultural integration. Religious services were substantially modernized—shortened and read in the vernacular with uncovered head and accompanied by the organ. Rituals and ceremonial laws that tended to segregate the Jews were ignored or altered. Germany, the center of Reform Judaism, was producing scholars and rabbis whose research and synods created a systematic theology to support the movement: Judaism, as an evolutionary and progressive religion, had freed itself from the restrictions of its more primitive, national past; its mission was now universal, to bring the message of social justice and brotherhood to mankind.

The breakup of traditional Jewish society was expressed in a variety of ways. Jewish modernists in Germany directed the poor youth of the cities and villages into vocational trades and agriculture. They sought to place communal organization on a voluntary basis and divest it of all its nonreligious functions. Among eastern European Jewry the new attitudes inspired a remarkable outpouring of political and cultural activity. Zionism (the movement to reestablish a Jewish homeland) and socialism, with their numerous factions, splits, and combinations, developed into full-grown organizations and challenged the bastions of traditional Judaism. A secular literature in Hebrew, Yiddish, and Russian found avid readers.

Some of those who emigrated to the United States embraced the new ideologies that were fragmenting the group in Europe. Nevertheless, until well into the 20th century the majority of the immigrants could recall, or had come directly from, a traditional Jewish society. The communal thrust of Judaism—the sense of being a community of fate, the discipline imposed by the halacha, and the obligation to brethren in distress —was still at the heart of their religio-ethnic outlook. Whatever their land of origin, American Jews saw themselves as part of Kelal Yisrael, the totality of Israel.

The younger and more adventurous, with fewer commitments to family and community, constituted a significant proportion of the immigrants; not many established·leaders came. Freedom, tolerance, and the promise of material reward for the deserving individual struck a responsive chord among the immigrants and their descendants. From the start there was tension between individual integration in the larger society and group continuity, and questions of self-definition were important.

From a tiny outpost at the edge of the Jewish world, the United States became the largest Jewish population center in the world. In 1978 an estimated 40 percent of the world Jewish population resided in the United States, compared with 21 percent in Israel. The great migration movement from east to west explains this development only in part. Six million of the 9 million Jews who lived in Europe on the eve of World War II perished in the Nazi holocaust. Suddenly and traumatically, American Jewry became the major center with the numbers and means to aid fellow Jews in peril.

THE COLONIAL
AND EARLY NATIONAL PERIODS

The Sephardic Jews who settled on the North American continent during the colonial period were part of the Iberian-Jewish diaspora created by the 15th- and 16th-century expulsions from Spain and Portugal. One stream of Sephardim found havens in the rising commercial centers of Holland, England, and their colonies, where they were well prepared for a pioneering role. Being by necessity geographically mobile, they settled, migrated, and resettled along the colonial trade routes and adapted their mercantile skills to the needs of international trade and a frontier economy. Concentrated in urban centers, they succeeded in establishing small but viable Jewish communities. Their tradition also encouraged cultural flexibility. They retained pride in their civilization that had flourished during the golden age of Spain, when their forefathers had combined Hebraic and secular learning and had served both the state and their people with distinction.

In the New World, Sephardic influences dominated the five congregations established in the port cities of New York (1656), Newport (1677), Savannah (1733), Philadelphia (1745), and Charleston (1750), links in a chain of settlements extending to the Dutch and English West Indies and anchored in the parent community in Amsterdam and the smaller but increasingly important community in London. The first Jewish refugees to arrive in New Amsterdam were threatened with expulsion because of their religion. They petitioned their brethren in Amsterdam to intercede, and Jewish shareholders of the Dutch West India Company used their influence to establish a more tolerant immigration policy. The immigrants' questions of religious law were occasionally submitted to the rabbinical courts of London and Amsterdam. When the less affluent mainland communities wanted to build a synagogue, they turned for aid—in the words of the 1729 appeal of New York's Shearith Israel (Remnant of Israel) congregation —to "kindred Sephardi congregations in Central and South America and Europe." In 1750 Newport's Jews received contributions for that purpose from the congregations of Jamaica, Surinam, Curaçao, and London. But above all, trade and family ties reinforced the connections among the scattered Sephardi settlements of the colonial world. Merchant families such as the Lopezes, Gomezes, Hendrickses, Seixases, and Riveras were related through marriage with branches scattered from Newport to Savannah. Individual members went on business to London and to the Caribbean, and the few new arrivals who continued to reach the mainland colonies from Amsterdam and London by way of the Dutch or English West Indies sustained the bonds of religion, culture, and economic interests until well into the 18th century.

The Ashkenazi Jews who settled in colonial America came from widely dispersed points in central and eastern Europe, often with London as a way-station. Ashkenazi families sometimes settled in London and sent relatives to America in the interest of family business, and immigrants, once established in the colonies, occasionally brought kinsmen from Europe, but chain migration did not develop. Those who crossed the ocean were by and large young, unmarried, and predisposed to adjust readily and individually to new conditions and join the Sephardi communities already there.

The fusion of the two groups in America was surprising. The Ashkenazi ritual differed from the Sephardi in style, pronunciation of the Hebrew, and liturgy. Furthermore, the first-generation Ashkenazim retained something of their own culture, reflected in a considerable body of correspondence in Yiddish. Nevertheless, Ashkenazim were among the leaders and main financial supporters of the colonial congregations. Moses Gomez, a Sephardi who presided over the Jewish community in New York in the first half of 1729, was followed by Jacob Franks (1688–1769), an Ashkenazi, in the second half. Two of the three trustees who acquired the site for the Newport synagogue in 1759 were Ashkenazim. The two groups intermarried with increasing frequency, despite occasional evidence of Sephardi hauteur. The sparseness of the Jewish population undoubtedly encouraged intermarriage, because for many the unacceptable alternative was to marry outside the faith. The occupational structure of the two groups was similar, and ethnic business ties quickly brought Ashkenazim and Sephardim together. The absence of authoritative religious leaders (the first ordained rabbis came to the United States in the 1840s) and the pace of Americanization also encouraged homogeneity.

The first small congregations met the full range of Jewish communal and religious needs. In addition to performing religious services, they maintained a school and a *mikveh* (ritual bath), supervised the supply of kosher meat, provided *matzot* (unleavened bread) for Passover, and either owned or cared for a cemetery. The synagogue accepted responsibility for the needy and supplied lodging for itinerants and medical care and burial services for the indigent.

The lay head of the synagogue (*parnass*) and the trustees endeavored to impose traditional norms of religious behavior upon their members with mixed success. Before a marriage could be performed, the approval of the parnass and sometimes of the trustees was needed. This was denied if one partner to the marriage was not Jewish. But sanctions such as fines, loss of synagogue honors, and denial of burial rights as a means of enforcing religious observance became less and less effective. In time both Shearith Israel and Philadelphia's Mikveh Israel (Hope of Israel) allowed the Jewish spouses of mixed marriages to be seatholders in the synagogue. Synagogue policy continued to be formally traditional and authoritarian but in practice it was indulgent toward the nonobservant.

Jewish identity was not a serious obstacle to participation in the larger society. As merchants and artisans, Jews provided necessary services. The decline of piety, the rise of deistic ideas, and the crystallization of American republicanism eased the way for Jews who wished to take part in public affairs. The Swedish naturalist Peter Kalm wrote as early as 1748 that Jews "enjoyed all the privileges common to other inhabitants." He also observed that they ate no pork, forbidden food for the observant Jew, but that "many of them (especially the young) when travelling did not make the least difficulty about eating this or any other meat." Thirty years later a Hessian officer wrote that the Jews in Newport "enjoy all the rights of citizenship. But unlike our Jews they are not distinguishable by their beards and attire . . . while their women wear the same French finery as the women of other faiths." The wills of New York Jews reflected amicable relationships with non-Jews. Of the 41 extant wills, 23 are witnessed only by Gentiles, and 12 by both Jews and Gentiles. Jews were not denied honorific appointments. In 1768 Moses Michael Hays (1739–1805) of Newport was chosen deputy inspector general of masonry for North America. Myer Myers (1723–1795) of New York was elected president of the Silversmith's Society in 1776 and again in 1786. Gershom Mendes Seixas (1746–

1816), minister of Shearith Israel, was appointed a trustee of Columbia College, then a Christian denominational institution, in 1784. In Philadelphia's grand procession to celebrate Pennsylvania's ratification of the United States Constitution, Benjamin Rush reported, "Pains were taken to connect Ministers of the most dissimilar religious principles together, thereby to show the influence of a free government in promoting Christian charity. The Rabbi of the Jews, locked in the arms of two ministers of the gospel, was a most delightful sight."

Although stereotypical anti-Jewish remarks occasionally appeared in the press and in public utterances, they reflected traditional prejudices rather than grave social mistreatment. Jews of standing joined clubs, charities, and private libraries along with their Christian peers and sent their children to the same schools. The daughter of the wealthy and observant Jacob Franks (1688–1769), pillar of Shearith Israel, married a DeLancey; his son married a Philadelphia Evans. In the 1790s Dr. David Nassy, a Philadelphia Jewish physician and scientist, replied to an accusation of Jewish self-segregation, "There are the Maraches, the Amrings, the Cohens, the Hombergs, the Wallachs, the Solises and several other families lawfully married to Christian women who go to their own churches, the men going to their synagogues, and who, when together, frequent the best society."

Jews did at first face civic and political disabilities derived from restrictions on religious dissenters, but even before the Revolution they had gradually acquired the privileges of domicile, trade, and religious organization. New York granted individual Jews citizenship: they voted and held minor appointive offices. Pennsylvania statutes that forbade Jews from holding public worship and restricted their commercial activities were not enforced.

Other colonies eager for commercial growth also al lowed Jews to establish permanent settlements. The colonies either granted citizenship or ignored the question altogether. The growth of dissenting Christian denominations eased the way for the Jews as well. In 1740 Parliament recognized this reality by formally granting Jewish aliens in the colonies the right to be naturalized after seven years of residence and exempting them from taking the oath "upon the true faith of a Christian."

The American Revolution legitimized the set of rights and ad hoc privileges that individual Jews had won. Only minor disabilities remained in those states whose constitutions required religious tests for public office. Most of the Jewish population had taken part in the struggle for independence; they had served in the army and distinguished themselves in battle. Jewish purveyors, merchant shippers, and financiers were in constant contact with government officials. Like the churches, the synagogues held special days of prayer and thanksgiving, issued petitions, and presented addresses to the political leaders and bodies of the republic. The Mikveh Israel Congregation petitioned the Commonwealth of Pennsylvania and the Constitutional Convention to remove religious restrictions on holding office and were gratified by the clause against religious tests and by the First Amendment's "no establishment of religion" proviso.

By the end of the century a largely native-born American Jewry participated in an increasingly open society. Even its Old Testament Hebraism formed part of the common American heritage. Biblical imagery reverberated equally in the congratulatory addresses sent by the Hebrew congregations to George Washington and in his replies. But by the first decades of the next century this high degree of integration began to raise a quite different question: would the American Jews be able to survive as a distinct entity? Of the five congregations that existed in 1776, one (Newport) had dissolved; fifty years later one new one (Richmond) had been established, and the two preeminent synagogues (Philadelphia and New York) had suffered secessions. When Shearith Israel's minister of 48 years, an energetic man of limited Hebraic learning, died in 1816 his place was assumed by a merchant who continued his own business activities and served as *hazzan* (reader) on a part-time basis.

Mordecai M. Noah (1785–1851), born in Philadelphia of mixed Sephardi-Ashkenazi stock (his maternal grandmother was Sephardi) was probably the best-known Jewish public figure in the first half of the 19th century. He settled in New York after serving from 1813 to 1815 as U.S. consul in Tunis, from where he was recalled by Secretary of State James Monroe because his religion formed an "obstacle to the exercise of [his] consular functions" and because of alleged mismanagement of funds. In 1818 when Shearith Israel rededicated its synagogue, Noah delivered the main address. He became a stormy figure in New York Democratic party politics, served for a time as editor of the *National Advocate*, and held the posts of sheriff (1822), grand sachem of Tammany (1824), and judge of the court of sessions (1841). In the 1830s, he edited and published the *Evening Star*, a Whig paper, and supported the anti-immigrant and anti-Catholic Native American party. He was a prolific playwright; five of his plays were produced between 1819 and 1822. For many years he also headed the most important Jewish charity, the Hebrew Benevolent Society.

Moved by the condition of North African Jewry, as well as by his own romanticism, Noah undertook to establish a "city of refuge for the Jews." In 1825, with the aid of friends, he purchased Grand Island in the Niagara River and renamed it Ararat. In an impressive dedication staged in the presence of militia, the Masons, local Indians (supposedly survivors of the ten lost tribes of Israel), and government officials, Noah proclaimed himself "Governor and Judge of Israel," offering the Jews of the world an asylum until "that great and final restoration to their ancient heritage." In 1844 he published his *Discourse on the Restoration of the Jews*, which called on the free peoples of the world, particularly Americans, to aid in the restoration of Zion.

THE GERMAN MIGRATION, 1830–1880

Second synagogues, established in Philadelphia in 1802 and in New York in 1825, were a harbinger of changes to come in American Jewry. In both cities the recently arrived Ashkenazi immigrants regarded the American Sephardic ritual, the social distance between themselves and the native-born, and religious laxity as sufficient justification for establishing themselves in separate congregations. After that, consensual restraints no longer prevented the multiplication of synagogues. The stimulus for further diversity became apparent in the mid-1830s when more and more immigrants arrived in families and groups of families having common ties in particular Old World localities. Ten years after New York's initial secession, the two synagogues had grown to ten.

Jews spread across the continent, forming the map of Jewish communities essentially as it is today. By the Civil War, 160 places had a Jewish communal life. San Francisco had a Jewish population two-thirds the size of Philadelphia's. Most of these immigrants were from Bavaria, Baden, Württemberg, and Posen, who left because of repressive legislation and the disruption of the agricultural peasant economy. They came from small hamlets and market towns where they had been petty tradesmen and dealers in cattle and where they were burdened by humiliating taxes and severe limitations on their right to marry, find employment, and establish domiciles. Consequently most of the immigrants were young and unmarried. Records from Württemberg show that between 1848 and 1855 62 percent of the emigrants were between 11 and 20, and 70 percent were under 31. Though products of a traditional Jewish milieu, they had only a meager religious and secular education. Those from Posen came from sizable, compact Jewish communities with a more learned and rigorous religious leadership and an artisan class. Smaller, but influential, groups came from England, Holland, and Bohemia, where Jews had moved toward political and cultural integration by the 1840s. These groups supplied most of the small number of professionals and intellectuals.

Although entire families sometimes emigrated— Simon and Rachel Guggenheim and their 12 children provide a celebrated example—more often a family would send a single son, with the understanding that at the first opportunity he would arrange for the rest to follow. Joseph Seligman (1819–1880), the founder of one of the leading post–Civil War American investment houses, left Bavaria in 1837 at the age of 17, sent for his two oldest brothers in 1839, and for a fourth brother in 1841. By 1843 seven more brothers and sisters and a widowed father had been brought over. The Seligmans were more famous than the others, and there were more of them, but otherwise they were typical of this youth-led family chain migration.

The Jews were part of the German migration, and, despite religious differences and historic prejudices, were drawn into the German social and cultural milieu in the United States. But Jews from the same town or region often banded together and traveled as a group, sometimes taking with them the Torah scroll and other religious objects needed for the future congregation and making special arrangements for kosher food during the journey.

The age, family structure, ethnic ties, and European experience of the Jewish immigrants equipped them for successful integration into the expanding American economy. The rapidly growing cities of the East, particularly the ports of entry, provided opportunities for tradesmen and small merchants. New York City's population grew from 166,000 in 1825 to 805,000 in 1860, while its Jewish population rose from approximately 500 to 40,000. The Jews engaged in tailoring and shoe-making and dealt in second-hand clothes and dry goods—occupations brought from Europe. A New York merchant's reference guide for 1859 listed 141 wholesale firms with Jewish names, all connected with some branch of the garment industry. A quarter of the gainfully employed immigrants from Poland—mostly Posen Jews—were tailors.

Peddling, however, was the most frequent means of making a living. At a time when there were few retail stores outside of the large cities, peddling filled a vital function in bringing the city's goods to the country-side. Immigrants purchased their supplies in New York and left on rural routes for a week or more or faced the fierce competition of the city's neighborhoods. Better opportunities existed where the distribution network was less developed. In 1855, 59 percent of the gainfully employed Jews of Easton, Pennsylvania, were peddlers.

Peddlers needed little or no initial capital, because they began their business entirely on credit; when they accumulated enough money, they moved from pack peddler to wagon peddler and then to store owner. The nexus of peddler, supplier-creditor, dry-goods retailer, wholesaler, clothing manufacturer, and importer evolved quickly, with German Jews playing a central role. Because credit was crucial to the system, family ties were of paramount importance. Relatives in New York or Cincinnati sent goods to the South or Far West that they would not risk to strangers. The expanding distribution network required clerks, bookkeepers, and skilled factory workers, also drawn from among immigrant relatives or countrymen. By the 1850s Jews in Milwaukee, Chicago, and Cincinnati had entered the meat-packing industry, and the largest wholesale shoe firm in the country, with outlets in Boston, Memphis, and St. Louis, was owned by the Friedmann family.

The growth of the distributive system shaped the map of Jewish settlement. The main transportation routes to the West became the sites of the new communities in the 1830s and 1840s. The first clusters of peddlers established themselves in inland cities like Albany (early 1830s) and Rochester, New York (early 1840s), Cleveland (1839), Chicago (1845), Milwaukee (1844), and St. Louis (1837). Within three or four years the first Jewish retail stores or peddler-supply depots opened, additional family members and countrymen came, and a congregation was established. By the 1850s such centers had satellite communities.

Cincinnati, an early crossroads for westward-bound travelers, the most important inland river port serving the Ohio River system, and a region with a large German population, attracted many Jewish immigrants. Its Jewish population grew to 3,300 in 1850 and to 10,000 in 1860. Its most influential synagogue was founded by peddlers, who by the 1850s had moved up to the retail clothing trade and had turned Cincinnati into a center for clothing manufacture. In 1855 its fifth synagogue was established, a Jewish hospital and benevolent-aid society had been founded, and two weeklies, one in English and one in German, went to subscribers throughout the region. Two of the preeminent rabbis in the country, Isaac Mayer Wise (1819–1900) and Max Lilienthal (1815–1882), held pulpits in the city. Cincinnati was the religious center for small communities throughout Indiana, Illinois, Tennessee, Kentucky, and Missouri. When Jewish merchants grew wealthy, they frequently sold their stores to younger brothers or relatives and moved to Cincinnati.

Jewish settlers also penetrated the South and the Far West, where regional differences affected the character of their economic and communal life. In the South, the path to success led from peddling to serving the commercial needs of the plantation economy as commission merchants and cotton brokers. New Orleans and Mobile and Montgomery, Alabama, were representative of the small to medium-sized provincial communities. The structure of southern white society undoubtedly contributed to the survival of such isolated communities.

In the Far West, on the other hand, the boom that followed the discovery of gold in California resulted in the extraordinarily swift growth of San Francisco. By the mid-1850s the city had about 4,000 Jews, and by the end of the decade, a third more. Open and fluid social and economic conditions and the absence of an established elite provided the Jews with an opportunity to enter many more fields and to participate in civic life. In the first two decades, most Jews established themselves as merchants and wholesalers, often representing family concerns in the East. Jewish peddlers followed the prospectors into the mining towns of the Sierras, supplied them with clothes and tools, and established stores. Minuscule communities in towns such as Sacramento and Stockton established and maintained close ties with the Jewish community in San Francisco.

Congregation building and splitting were common in this period. As additional immigrants settled in a city, they strengthened the traditions of the initial group or introduced new ones. The original congregation, which generally included a bloc from Bavaria and Posen and a scattering of Bohemian, English, and Dutch Jews, usually divided into German and Polish congregations; then, if the population was large enough, as it was in New York, the proliferation continued. The splintering was largely social and cultural rather than doctrinal. The founders of the new congregations, laymen with a rudimentary religious background, simply wanted to maintain as best they could the cherished customs of home.

In the mid-1840s an additional factor contributed to fragmentation. In the more established synagogues, demands were made for minor innovations in the conduct of the services, although this did not imply a radical revision of traditional practice based on a new interpretation of Judaism. The changes, although rarely stated in those terms, reflected a desire to Americanize the synagogue with a more decorous service and an English sermon rather than a German one or none at all.

The arrival in the 1840s of the first ordained rabbis, by and large university-trained, added an ideological dimension. They brought the prestige of their religious station and their academic title, for ordination carried with it the authority to interpret religious law. For the traditionalists, this meant a rigorously conservative rendering of the halacha, but the immigrant rabbis, sympathizers or outright advocates of Reform Judaism, used their authority to legitimize the Reformist trends. They easily replaced or absorbed into their ranks the Jewish minister, a peculiarly American creation. The minister had evolved from the hazzan, who led the congregation in worship, a function any religiously observant Jew literate in Hebrew was allowed to fill. The professionalization of the hazzan had resulted in part from the paucity of qualified laymen, in part from the absence of rabbis. Influenced, too, by the Protestant model, he added preaching to his duties and assumed the title of minister.

One of these ministers, Isaac Leeser (1806–1868) became the spokesman for traditional Judaism and the first national leader in American Jewish life. Born in Westphalia, in Germany, where he received some Judaic and secular education, Leeser served as minister of Philadelphia's Congregation Mikveh Israel from 1829 to 1850. He founded the first American Jewish periodical, *The Occident*, in 1843, published a number of Jewish educational primers intended for a nationwide audience, and established a short-lived publishing house and rabbinical college.

Leeser's effort to create a "union of all Israelites in America" in 1841 was prompted by the accusation of ritual murder leveled against a group of Syrian Jews, which had become an international incident. For the first time American Jewry acted in concert, holding public meetings, enlisting the support of non-Jews, and calling on the U.S. government to intercede. Leeser emerged as the leading figure in the protest movement, but the momentum created by the collaborative effort was not enough to establish a permanent, representative organization. A central organization of sorts, the Board of Delegates of American Israelites, was founded in 1859, again using the impetus from protests over the violation of Jewish rights abroad, this time the case of a Jewish infant in Italy, who was baptized without the knowledge of his parents and abducted by papal guards to be raised as a Christian. Leeser tried to broaden both the constituency and the scope of the board, but the increasingly rancorous debate over religious reform absorbed the energies of its other leaders.

All through the 1850s and 1860s, efforts to establish a

synod, issue a standard prayerbook, agree upon a set of guiding principles, create a federation of synagogues, and establish a theological seminary failed in the face of theological dispute and personal feuds. Cincinnati's Isaac Wise, a moderate Reform Jew, was a diligent compromiser and improviser in religious principles as well as in practice. Born in Bohemia, Wise received training in a Talmudic academy and probably also attended a university. After a brief ministry in a small provincial town, he emigrated to the United States, served as rabbi in Albany, New York, and was then called in 1854 to the wealthy B'nai Jeshurun in Cincinnati, which he turned into a base for his larger ambitions. To the theological left of Wise, David Einhorn (1809–1879) presented a radical and ideologically consistent view of Judaism. Einhorn arrived in the United States in 1855, already one of the established leaders of the radical Reform wing in Germany. He had little patience with piecemeal efforts to modify old practices or with Wise's inconsistencies and compromises. No all-embracing framework could include the Leeser, Wise, and Einhorn factions.

Polemics and negotiations eventually resulted in the crystallization of a Reform denomination, although it was not the comprehensive liberal-traditional Judaism some had hoped for. On the congregational level, pragmatic laymen fitted their practices to the Reform style and paid little attention to theological controversies; Wise's flexibility and organizational ability gave the movement institutional form. In 1873 he established the Union of American Hebrew Congregations

(UAHC), which soon absorbed the Board of Delegates of American Israelites. Two years later, the UAHC opened Hebrew Union College in Cincinnati, the first seminary established in the United States to train rabbis, with Wise as its president. By 1880 most American synagogues, aside from those established by the newly arriving east European immigrants, were Reform.

Ideological positions were also clarified. In 1885, Kaufmann Kohler (1843–1926), son-in-law and spiritual heir of Einhorn, convened a conference of rabbis and formulated a Reform platform that included the radical position that had been the source of contention twenty years earlier. The Jews were no longer a nation, the platform declared: they were a religious community. Judaism was a "progressive religion ever striving to be in accord with the postulates of reason." Of the "Mosaic legislation," only its moral laws and the ceremonials that "elevate and sanctify our lives" were binding. The rabbis called on all men of good will to establish "the reign of truth and righteousness among men."

The pronouncement indicated both the astonishingly rapid acculturation of the German Jews and the prompt acceptance by their ministers of advanced social theories. Scarcely a generation after their arrival, they had reformulated their Jewish identity in terms of the congenial model of late-19th-century liberal American Protestantism. Their congregations—now called temples—expressed their middle-class propriety. Elaborate structures and the distinguished and well-paid rabbis who preached from their pulpits bore witness to their affluence. Brief and decorous services, almost exclusively in English and accompanied by choir and organ, lightened the burden of attendance.

Some carried the radical teachings of Reform one step further. Felix Adler (1851–1933), trained for the rabbinate and son of an American Reform leader, concluding that Judaism was too confining in the pursuit of a universalistic humanism, founded the Ethical Culture Society in 1876. Charles Fleischer, rabbi of Boston's Temple Israel, severed his ties with his temple and began to preach a religion of democracy around 1900.

Philanthropy offered another avenue for expressing ethnic identity. The first relief societies had functioned under the auspices of the synagogue, then they became autonomous, then completely independent. Initially serving only the poor among the congregation, they later aided the Jewish poor of an entire city. Immigration increased the number of impoverished Jews, many of whom were not affiliated with synagogues, but the associations accepted members regardless of their affiliation. By the 1870s the larger Jewish settlements had a variety of benevolent societies, some with broad community support and others based on old-country origin or on a particular philanthropic function. The wretched conditions of the public charitable institutions and the fact that most were sponsored by Christian denominations—raising the fear of proselytizing—led to the establishment of the first large welfare institutions: orphanages, hospitals, homes for the aged, and schools for the poor. Jewish hospitals were opened in Cincinnati (1850), in New York (1852), in Philadelphia (1865), and in Chicago (1868). Orphan asylums were founded in Charleston, South Carolina (1801), in Philadelphia (1855), in New York (1859), and in Cleveland (1868). As the dimensions of the undertakings grew, so did the trend toward consolidation among some of the societies. In the larger communities "united Hebrew charities" came into existence in the 1860s and 1870s.

Women came to play a significant part in these undertakings. At first their separate charity organizations were attached to individual synagogues, but in time women established community-wide social-service societies. Rebecca Gratz (1781–1869) pioneered the first Jewish Sunday school in Philadelphia in 1838. Women in other cities followed her lead, making the education of children their special preserve. These activities marked the first stirrings of a separate role for women in Jewish public life.

Mutual-aid societies underwent a similar process of dissociation from religious groups. Although synagogues retained control over some of them, most of the offshoots of the traditional sick-visitation and burial societies were able to survive the congregational splintering only by asserting their independence. That step also opened their doors to the growing numbers of Jews who were only casual attendants of the synagogue or no longer religiously observant.

Influenced by American models, the mutual-aid society developed into the lodge and fraternal order. Twenty-five years after its founding, the Order of B'nai

B'rith was a national organization dedicated to "uniting Israelites in the work of promoting their highest interests and those of humanity," with a membership of over 20,000. Along with the other orders, it responded to the needs of Jews who had encountered discrimination in general orders like the Odd Fellows and the Masons.

The Jewish fraternal orders, with their secret rites, special regalia, and mottoes, offered an American aura denied them elsewhere and supplied the mutual aid and fellowship no longer provided by the factional synagogues. They also accepted communal responsibilities, sponsored charitable projects, and organized to fight prejudice. Social and literary societies mushroomed and in the 1870s acquired an institutional form in the Young Men's Hebrew Associations (YMHA), which began to appear in the larger cities. In all these activities the thrust of acculturation also led to social discrimination. The B'nai B'rith and YMHA in their early years did not welcome eastern European newcomers.

On the eve of the mass migration from eastern Europe, American Jewry was relatively homogeneous. The large German Jewish group had absorbed both the native-born community it found on arrival and the Posen, Bohemian, and other Jews, including the early arrivals from eastern Europe, who followed. Congregations established in the 1850s because the existing ones were too liberal or too German were, by the 1880s, affiliated with the Reform movement. Reform Judaism's prescriptive demands were minimal, and it offered no obstacles to a broad range of essentially secular associational activities. Thus diversity did not become divisive. The importance of German culture in the social and intellectual life of the group was an integrating force of another kind. Jewish social clubs and literary societies reflected strong German influence. German Jews subscribed to and wrote for the German-language press and were patrons of the German-language theater. Some Jews completely identified with the German ethnic group, while others maintained a "triple loyalty," as expressed by the Chicago rabbi Bernhard Felsenthal (1822–1908): "Racially I am a Jew, for I have been born among the Jewish nation. Politically I am an American as patriotic, as enthusiastic, as devoted an American citizen as it is possible to be. But spiritually I am a German, for my inner life has been profoundly influenced by Schiller, Goethe, Kant, and other intellectual giants of Germany."

Between 1860 and 1880 a Jewish business elite appeared. Its leaders were the investment bankers, department-store innovators, clothing manufacturers, and metals, shoe-manufacturing, and meat-processing entrepreneurs. The family business pattern that had brought mercantile success in the 1850s had created large fortunes by the 1880s. The German Jewish patrician class in New York—closely knit by ethnic, social, and family bonds and by business dealings—was especially striking. It was also linked by social ties and business interests to its counterparts across the country.

As New York rose to financial preeminence, it attracted families who at first had local business outlets there and who then moved into finance or large-scale merchandising. Kuhn, Loeb and Company and Heidelbach, Ickelheimer and Company were run by Cincinnati merchant families who opened New York branches of their clothing and wholesale firms and then entered investment banking. The Lehman brothers— Emanuel (1827–1907), Henry (1821–1855), and Mayer (1830–1897)—who were originally cotton factors in the South, followed a similar path. By the 1850s their cotton brokerage firm required a New York branch; after the Civil War the brothers transferred their activities to New York, extended their commodity dealings, then entered investment banking. The Straus family—Lazarus (1809–1898) and his sons, Isidor (1845–1912), Nathan (1848–1931), and Oscar (1850–1926)—moved from Talbotton, Georgia, to New York in 1866. By the 1880s Isidor and Nathan were partners in the drygoods business of R. H. Macy and Company, which they turned into a giant department store.

The eight Seligman brothers moved from peddling to retailing, branched out from the South, and in 1847 opened an importing house in New York. The discovery of gold in California led Jesse (1827–1894) and Leopold (1831–1862) to set up a store in San Francisco in 1850. Two years later they began consigning gold, for reshipment to foreign markets, to the New York office headed by Joseph. During the Civil War the brothers underwrote U.S. bonds and supplied the Union Army with uniforms. When it ended, they turned from dry goods and clothing manufacture to international investment banking with branches in London, Paris, Frankfurt, San Francisco, and New Orleans, each branch headed by a brother.

In other cities men like Adam Gimbel (1817–1896), Louis Bamberger (1855–1944), Edward A. Filene (1860–1937), and Julius Rosenwald (1862–1932) revolutionized American retailing. German Jews held a commanding position in the clothing trades. In New York 80 percent of all retail and 90 percent of all wholesale clothing firms were owned by Jews; in the rest of the country the figure was only slightly less. A U.S. Census report in 1890 provides some notion of the general affluence of American Jews. Bankers, brokers, and wholesale merchants represented 15 percent; retail dealers, about 35 percent; accountants, bookkeepers, and clerks, 17 percent; salesmen, agents, and auctioneers, about 12 percent; professionals, 5 percent; skilled workers, about 12 percent; tailors, 3 percent; and peddlers, only 1 percent.

For the German Jews, all that remained was to achieve an acceptance in society commensurate with their economic and cultural success. But the appearance of impoverished, Yiddish-speaking immigrants from eastern Europe—about 30,000 of them between 1870 and 1880, and immensely larger numbers soon after—threatened the standing the American Jews had attained.

MIGRATION FROM EASTERN EUROPE, 1881–1924

In 1880 perhaps one-sixth of the 250,000 American Jews were immigrants from eastern Europe. Forty years later they and their children constituted about five-sixths of the 4 million Jews in the United States. One-third of eastern European Jewry left their homes during those decades, and over 90 percent of them came to the United States. This largest of Jewish population movements radically altered the demography, social structure, cultural life, and communal order of American Jewry.

Several factors combined to cause this mass exodus. A high birthrate and relatively low death rate increased the Jewish population of eastern Europe from approximately 1.5 million in 1800 to 6.8 million in 1900, all within the confining pales of Jewish settlement. Seventy-five percent of the immigrants were from the Russian Pale, which consisted of the 15 western provinces of European Russia and the 10 provinces of Congress (that is, Russian-held) Poland. The Pale constituted about 20 percent of the regions then within the borders of European Russia. All but a privileged few were forbidden to live outside the Pale, and within, restrictive laws further limited Jews to residence in towns and cities.

Another 18 percent of the immigrants came from Galicia, Bukovina, and Hungary, all regions of Austria-Hungary. The Hapsburg government had granted civil

Central Europe

500   Km.   Miles

Leningrad
(St. Petersburg)
St. Petersberg

STONIAN
S.S.R.
Estonia

Livonia

ga
S.S.R.

Vitebsk

Moscow

Russian Empire

RUSSIAN S.F.S.R.

o
ius
a

Minsk
Minsk

Smolensk

Mogilev

Volga

no
no
ELORUSSIAN
S.S.R.   **U.**   **S.**   **S.**   **R.**

Chernigov

olhynia

Kiev
Kiev

Poltava

Kharkov
Poltava

Podolia

Dnieper

UKRAINIAN S.S.R.

Don

MOLDAVIAN
S.S.R.
Kishinev

Ekaterinoslav

Kherson

a

Bessarabia

Kherson

Taurida

Odessa

Sea of Azov

A

Crimea

arest

Black Sea

IA

İstanbul

TURKEY

Jewish Pale of Settlement in the Russian Empire

Boundary of the Congress Kingdom of Poland, 1815–1863

Boundary of the Hungarian Kingdom before 1918

rights to the Jews in the 1860s, but local circumstances conspired to create a repressive situation, though it was less marked by the open violence that was common elsewhere. Only 4 percent of the immigrants were from Romania, where the proportion of emigrating Jews to Jewish population was as high as in Russia. The Jews in Romania lived under essentially the same conditions as in the Russian Pale: no civil rights, ruinous restrictions on trading, and periodic expulsion from towns and villages.

Economic and social changes upset the Jewish occupational structure and further stimulated departure. In the 1870s industrialization and modern agriculture began to displace the petty merchants, peddlers, artisans, teamsters, factors, and innkeepers. After the assassination of Tsar Alexander II in 1881, the new regime introduced policies that encouraged mob violence. Pogroms in 1881 and 1882 struck over 200 Jewish communities and ushered in three decades of anti-Jewish outbursts. An economic policy of pauperization—the infamous May Laws of 1882—included the expulsion of the Jews from villages and rural centers and severe restrictions on their trade in the cities. In 1900 no province in the Pale had less than 14 percent of its Jews on relief, and in Vilna, Kovno, and other cities, more than one in four Jews received some form of charitable aid from the Jewish community.

The banishment of 20,000 Jews from Moscow in 1891 was followed by similar actions in St. Petersburg and Kharkov, the Kishinev Pogrom of 1903, the Russo-Japanese War, more pogroms in 1905, and the 1905 Revolution, all of which accelerated emigration. In one year, 1882, the 13,000 who arrived in the United States following the pogroms of 1881–1882 amounted to almost half the number that had arrived in the entire decade of the 1870s. In 1891 the number of immigrants climbed above 50,000 and then rose by 50 percent the following year in the wake of new disturbances in Russia. Jewish immigration rose from over 200,000 in the 1880s to 300,000 in the 1890s. From 1900 to 1914 another 1.5 million arrived, many of them the wives and children of the earlier immigrants. In seven of the ten years preceding the outbreak of World War I, over 100,000 Jews arrived annually. The peak year was 1906, when 152,000 Jews entered the country, 14 percent of the total immigration for that year.

Data from 1899 to 1914 indicate that the immigrants were generally young people who intended to settle permanently; a high proportion were skilled workers, they were drawn overwhelmingly from cities and towns, and they were part of a family migration. The age group 14 to 40 formed 70 percent of the immigrating Jews, compared with 47 percent of the Jewish population of Russia in that age group. Females were 44 percent, children under 14, 24 percent, all of which indicates a young family migration. The Russian Jewish father in his twenties or thirties preceding his family was typical. The family character of the migration also indicated an intention to remain in America. Between 1908 and 1924, for every 100 Jews arriving in the United States, 5 returned to Europe, as compared to 33 returnees for every 100 in the total immigration.

The Jewish immigration deviated from the norm also in occupational distribution. Of the gainfully employed, 64 percent were skilled workers, compared with about 20 percent for immigrants as a whole. Less than 40 percent of the gainfully employed Jewish population in Russia were skilled workers. The data for mercantile occupations—31 percent of gainfully employed Jews in Russia and 5.5 percent among Jews emigrating from Russia—indicates the self-selecting factor of the immigration. Of the young, skilled workers who left Russia, 60 percent were in the clothing trades. The rise of a Jewish clothing industry in the Pale of the Settlement—a result of the economic forces restructuring the eastern European economy—provided an intermediate stage for many on the move to the United States. Overflowing cities like Łódź, Warsaw, Vilna, and Białystok drew uprooted villagers, artisans, and laborers but offered only a precarious existence.

Jews from southern Russia crossed into Austria-Hungary, often surreptitiously, reached Vienna or Berlin, and then proceeded to one of the transatlantic ports —Hamburg, Bremen, Rotterdam, Amsterdam, or Antwerp. From western Russia, the route crossed the German border to Berlin and thence to the ports. Jewish emigrant-aid societies in Europe tried to direct and control the exodus, but overwhelmed by numbers, they provided mainly emergency assistance at critical transfer points. At the ports of entry in the United States, local relief societies met the ships, guided the arrivals through landing procedures, and provided aid and shelter when necessary. New York, the preeminent port of entry, developed a model organization for the purpose, the Hebrew Immigrant Aid Society (HIAS).

The German Jews had spread out across the land, turning cities like Cincinnati and San Francisco into major Jewish centers. The eastern European, or "Russian" Jews, as they were commonly called, crowded into the great cities of the East and Midwest, especially New York. Of the nearly 1.5 million Jews who landed in New York between 1881 and 1911, about 70 percent remained there. In 1860, the city sheltered 25 percent of the total Jewish population of the United States. In 1880 its share rose to about 33 percent, and four decades later to 45 percent. New York and the cities with the next two largest Jewish populations—Chicago and Philadelphia—accounted for 58 percent of the Jewish population. Seven other cities, all in the East and Midwest, accounted for another 14 percent. Probably 60 percent of American Jews could be found in the northeast corridor from Boston to Baltimore, another 30 percent in the main urban centers of the Midwest. The approximate proportion of Jews in the population of these cities in 1920 was New York (26 percent), Cleveland and Newark (13 percent each), Philadelphia (11 percent), Boston, Baltimore, and Pittsburgh (10 percent each), Chicago (9 percent), St. Louis (7 percent), and Detroit (6 percent).

Like other urban immigrants in the late 19th and early 20th centuries, Russian Jews crowded into ethnic enclaves. Chicago's West Side, Boston's North End, Philadelphia's downtown (South Philadelphia), and New York's Lower East Side were among the better known of these densely populated ghettos. Within the tight compass of the Jewish quarter, the immigrants found work, housing, and a network of familiar social and cultural institutions that offered continuity with the past and transition to the new life. In 1910, 540,000 Jews lived in the 1.5-square-mile area of the Lower East Side. In the typical five- or six-story tenement house, three- and four-room apartments housed families in which four or five children were common, and survival often required taking in a boarder as well. A 1908 survey of 250 East Side families showed that 50 percent slept three or four to a room; nearly 25 percent, five or more to a room; only 25 percent, two to a room. Though the Jews suffered a high rate of nervous disorders, suicides, and tuberculosis, they had a strikingly lower death rate than other immigrants.

A square block in the heart of any large ghetto held among its tenements the workshops of the garment trade, basement synagogues, saloons, and cafes. Workingmen, intellectuals, party functionaries and their followers, pious men, and an assortment of gamblers, prostitutes, *shtarke* (strong-arm men), and their clients rubbed shoulders.

Crime was of great concern to the immigrant community. *Noms de guerre,* such as Kid Twist, Yuski Nigger ("king of the horse poisoners"), Big Jack Zelig, Dopey Benny (a specialist in strike breaking), and Gyp the Blood, hid the identity of men like Max Zweibach, Joseph Toblinsky, William Albert, Benjamin Fein, and Harry Horowitz. These criminals operated almost exclusively in the Jewish quarter, extracting protection money from vulnerable Jewish merchants, gambling parlors, and houses of prostitution and supplying repeaters on election day and strikebreakers in industrial disputes.

Following every disclosure of vice or crime, the Yiddish press led the Jews in agonizing self-examination, playing on the theme that "the first generation to grow up under the free sky of America" had spawned the criminals. In 1902 German Jewish donors in New York City founded a Jewish Protectory and Aid Society to work with delinquents and prisoners. In 1912 the community established an investigatory bureau to collect evidence and cooperate with the authorities in combating crime in the Jewish neighborhoods. The number of Jewish felons was actually comparatively low, but they were very visible, and Jewish sensitivity made them even more so. In the 1920s, as conditions encouraged the growth of organized crime, criminals who had operated in the immigrant ghettos expanded their activities. Arnold Rothstein (1882–1928), son of a prominent member of New York's Orthodox Jewish community, became a leading underworld figure, and Louis "Lepke" Buchalter (1897–1944) headed the so-called Murder Inc. gang.

The associational strength of the immigrants was drawn from the clusters of fellow townsmen (*landsleit*) who sought one another out in the Jewish quarters. The landsleit met the immigrants' initial problems of adjustment through mutual aid. The vast majority of the 326 permanent congregations on the Lower East Side in 1907 were synagogues of landsleit, microcosms, so far as conditions permitted, of the old kehillahs. A 1917 study of the 365 Lower East Side congregations estimated that 90 percent owned cemetery plots, nearly half had free-loan societies, a third had sick-benefit societies, and nearly half sponsored traditional study groups. From the start, the landsleit also established separate societies or *landsmanshaftn,* which generally offered insurance, sick benefits, interest-free loans, and cemetery rights. They sent aid back to the home town and served as informal but effective employment agencies (contractors in the garment trades frequently recruited their workers from the landsleit). In 1917 about 1,000 such independent societies in New York had an aggregate membership of over 100,000.

Many of the landsmanshaftn found it financially advantageous to affiliate with a fraternal order. The Independent Order B'rith Abraham, one of a number, claimed a national membership of 182,000 in 1913. Regional groupings of landsmanshaftn into Polish, Galician, Romanian, and Sephardic confederations also formed to sponsor major philanthropic projects such as old-age homes, religious schools, hospitals, and orphan asylums. Through these sometimes complex undertakings, the landsmanshaftn introduced their members to American business practices and civic organization.

A newcomer's immediate need was a job. Most often he found it in one of the industries in the Jewish quarter, especially the clothing industry. In 1900 one out of every three Russian Jews employed in the major cities made his living in some branch of the garment trades.

A high degree of specialization in production allowed the immigrant to quickly master a subspecialty commensurate with his experience and physical stamina. Small contractors and subcontractors recruited their own labor forces and organized production in the lofts and tenement flats of the Jewish quarter. Poverty and long workdays—until the turn of the century a 70-hour week was not uncommon—made proximity of shop and home imperative.

Other ghetto industries were the tobacco-and-cigar industry, which accounted for 7 percent of Jewish employment, and home construction (usually renovating ghetto property), which accounted for 6 percent in 1900. Many were bakers. The slaughtering and dressing of meat became Jewish industries because of the ritual requirements of *kashruth*.

But the apparel trade, with its 60-percent share of the 60 percent of Russian Jews in industry, was the backbone of the Jewish neighborhood economy in New York, Boston, Philadelphia, Baltimore, and Chicago. In New York in 1880 almost all of the almost 1,000 major clothing manufacturers were German Jews: they employed 64,669 people. By 1913 the industry's 16,552 factories were largely owned by Russian Jews and employed 312,245 people, about three-quarters of whom were also Russian Jews.

A high percentage of single women employed as factory labor distinguished the Jewish working class from other immigrant working classes. In the garment industry, where most were concentrated, women received half the wages as men for similar work, a fact recognized and condemned by Jewish male coworkers. Once married, Jewish women left the factory but continued to contribute to the family's income by taking in boarders and engaging in petty retailing.

Jewish immigrant enclaves provided a range of entrepreneurial opportunities. In 1900 one-fifth of the gainfully employed Russian Jews were in mercantile trade; of these, a quarter were petty tradesmen and peddlers, and nearly half were proprietors of retail stores. A significant number acquired some measure of wealth. One reliable observer writing about New York in 1905 remarked: "Almost every newly arrived Russian Jewish laborer comes into contact with a Russian Jewish employer, almost every Russian tenement dweller must pay his exorbitant rent to a Jewish landlord." The Russian Jewish "fortunes" ranged between $25,000 and $200,000, he noted. Contracting in the apparel trades permitted the aspiring businessman to go into business with minimal capital by using family labor and a few hired workers. The chances of rising to manufacturer were slim, and the rate of business failures among manufacturers considerable, but it was an expanding industry, and the number of Russian Jewish clothing manufacturers nonetheless grew.

Real estate offered opportunities for those who had capital, access to credit, and willingness to invest in deteriorating property. The movement to newer neighborhoods after 1900 provided additional opportunities. By 1910 the class of retail merchants, proprietors of small businesses, white-collar workers, and professionals constituted a much larger share of the gainfully employed Jews than it had a decade before.

The newcomers who were religiously Orthodox—in all likelihood the majority of immigrants, at least when they arrived—transplanted their institutions and way of life with difficulty. In the towns they left, the traditional communal polity still exercised considerable control. Social movements and external pressures had weakened its consensual basis—a development more evident in the cities than in the towns—but the traditional structure was still intact. In education, charity, and religious needs, communal organization functioned well enough. In the United States, however, the very conditions of freedom and the absence of corporate group status, which the immigrants accepted gratefully, left only voluntary means for reestablishing their way of life. Various ideological movements competed freely for their loyalty, and fraternal orders, trade unions, cultural centers, and recreational enterprises offered alternatives to the synagogue community. A more direct confrontation to the Orthodox way of life was the economic necessity or opportunity of violating the Sabbath, so central to the Jewish religious culture.

The failure to re-create an authoritative religious leadership was a crucial element in the erosion of the Orthodox community, manifesting itself most critically in the decline of the rabbinate. In eastern Europe the rabbi's duties stemmed from his expertise in expounding the religious law that regulated Jewish civil life. He also served as arbitrator, overseer of public institutions, and scholar-teacher. In the United States his communal role atrophied. Supervising kashruth became a private, commercial undertaking, and the highly responsible function of adjudicating divorce cases now belonged to the state courts; granting a religious divorce, in fact, came perilously close to being a criminal act. At best, the rabbi found employment with a congregation that gave him no security, meager wages, and little authority. Most immigrant synagogues neither had the funds nor felt the need for a rabbi. Only rarely did a rabbi command the prestige and congregational support required to exert public authority in the religious life of the community.

Individual synagogues did develop broader constituencies during this period, drawing their members from a homeland region rather than from one particular town or city. They attracted larger, more acculturated, and more affluent memberships, acquired elaborate buildings, and called distinguished rabbis to their pulpits. Their lay leaders provided support for the few collaborative efforts mounted by the Orthodox community, of which religious education was the most difficult and perhaps the most important.

The conventional form of elementary schooling in eastern Europe was the *heder*, a class for boys of mixed ages, which met from early morning to dusk at the home of the teacher. Girls received no formal schooling, though some were instructed privately. The curriculum emphasized reading the prayerbook in Hebrew, studying the Pentateuch, and, for the more advanced, studying Biblical commentaries and the legal codes.

Social constraints and parental concern ensured high standards. In the United States the heder became a supplementary school that children attended after public-school hours, and in the absence of communal restraints, it soon degenerated. A 1909 survey of Jewish education in New York described a heder as meeting "in a room or two, in the basement or upper floor of some old dilapidated building where the rent is at a minimum." The masters were ill equipped, their approach to education sterile, and their "sole purpose to eke out some kind of livelihood." Reports from Chicago and Philadelphia confirmed the survey's overall conclusion.

The enervating struggle for survival in part explained the acquiescence of immigrant parents to this system, but the alacrity with which they embraced the public school and relegated religious education to an ancillary position also indicated a new set of priorities. The free state school promised material and social betterment; the heder provided the minimum Jewish continuity. Parental exhortations to the young to find success in the secular world heightened the conflict between the traditional culture and the American way.

Traditionalists tried to remedy the inadequacy of the heder by establishing parochial schools, Talmudic academies, and communal supplementary education, but in 1910 there were only two parochial schools and a small nucleus of an academy, all in New York. Orthodoxy had neither the money, the leadership, nor the will to support more.

The afternoon communal school proved most promising. Its origin was the European Talmud Torah, a charity school for those unable to afford tuition for the heder. In the United States it retained its charitable and consequently communal character. Popular support, public accountability, and larger enrollments led to better pedagogy and more effective management. A New York survey in 1909 recorded 14,000 children attending 468 heders, and 10,000 attending 22 Talmud Torah schools. As their superiority to the heder became apparent, the Talmud Torahs began to lose their stigma as charity schools. By the decade after 1910, all large immigrant centers had them, usually supported by the lay leaders of the larger, community-minded synagogues.

Despite these signs of renewal, Orthodoxy as guardian and moderator of transplanted east European Jewry lost its hegemony in the passage to the United States. Most immigrants retained some allegiance to tradition —synagogues overflowed on the High Holy Days, and enterprising religious functionaries organized services in hundreds of halls. Most children received some religious training, for which parents preferred the old-country form of education to the modern schools established in the immigrant quarters by Americanized Jews. In the 1920s successful Americanized immigrants moved out of the ghettos and established synagogues that were still traditional but more lenient and moderately innovative, a compromise between their American middle-class desire for social integration and their ties to the traditional culture.

Socialism and Zionism, the secular ideologies from

eastern Europe, opened new fissures within the communities, yet they also offered theories and programs that transcended ghetto parochialism. The ideologues and activists who were the pacesetters of these movements infused Yiddish culture with vitality and made it responsive to immigrant needs. The Yiddish press, theater, and literature were both polemical platforms and binding forces.

The Yiddish poets and prose writers—the "sweatshop school"—described the crushing, dehumanizing experience of industrial work. Morris Rosenfeld (1862–1923) wrote poems about the pain of never seeing his son awaken, of leaving for the shop while the child still slept and returning late at night. In 1907 a group of newly arrived immigrant writers dubbed the *Yunge* (young ones) launched another literary movement. More sophisticated than their predecessors and influenced by contemporary European trends, the poets Mani Leib (1884–1953) and H. Leivick (1886–1962) and the novelist Joseph Opatashu (1886–1954), wrote with an intimacy that reflected their weariness of high-flown rhetoric; they demanded art in place of propaganda. Other, still younger writers calling themselves the *In Zich* (introspectives) rebelled against the Yunge in the 1920s. Popular Yiddish novelists like Sholem Asch (1880–1957) and I. J. Singer (1893–1944), translated into English for American readers, achieved some popularity with their themes of Jewish life in eastern Europe and immigrant life in America.

Jacob Gordin (1853–1909) introduced serious drama to the Yiddish theater at the turn of the century and opened the way for others, such as David Pinski (1872–1959), whose works were produced by Max Rheinhardt in Germany, and Peretz Hirshbein (1880–1948). In the 1920s a revival of serious theater included experimental groups of merit. But the Yiddish theater was also recreation for the multitudes with its musicals and melodramatic potboilers—*White Slave, Love for Sale, Money, Love and Shame*. Benefit night, when organizations sold blocks of tickets, turned theater-going into a communal event. In New York in 1917 seven houses were presenting Yiddish plays, and Boston, Philadelphia, Baltimore, Chicago, and Los Angeles had Yiddish theaters. The spirited literary life of the Jewish quarter catered to all tastes and interests. Journals were launched and closed, literary feuds fought on the lecture circuit and in the newspapers, and, inevitably, politics and ideology left their imprint.

The immigrant community also developed a vigorous trade-union movement before World War I. Seasonal work, the decentralization into small plants and sweatshops, and continual turnover in manpower were long the bane of union organizers. Dual unionism and socialist factionalism further aggravated their difficulties. After 1900, however, increased immigration, experience, and a lessening of internal dissension provided a basis for expansion and consolidation of the unions. From 1909 to 1914 a series of massive strikes, often accompanied by brutality, in New York and Chicago transformed the unions into stable, aggressive organizations.

The "uprising of the twenty thousand" opened the

union era. Young Jewish and Italian girls—many in their teens—in the shirtwaist branch of the garment industry held out on strike from November 1909 to February 1910, despite the blows of hired thugs and the abuses of the police and the courts. Progressives and feminists aided the strikers. Wealthy New York women raised bail for the arrested girls, and Columbia Law School dean George W. Kirchway (1885–1942), among others, helped defend them in court. The cloak makers struck half a year later, an event styled "the great revolt." The chairman of the strike committee, Abraham Rosenberg (1870–1935), saw the thousands leaving the shops in response to the strike order: "I could only picture to myself such a scene taking place when the Jews were led out of Egypt." Peacemakers from the settlement houses and from the Jewish elite interceded. Lillian Wald (1867–1940) of the Henry Street Settlement, Henry Moskowitz (1879–1936) of the Madison Street Settlement, and the two leading figures in Jewish communal affairs, Jacob H. Schiff (1847–1920), head of Kuhn, Loeb and Company, and Louis Marshall (1856–1929) put pressure on the Russian Jewish manufacturers who refused to recognize the union. Through the efforts of Boston department store owner A. Lincoln Filene, Louis D. Brandeis (1856–1941), the lawyer and social reformer, entered the mediation effort and ended the strike. The 1910 Chicago strike in the men's clothing industry and others elsewhere followed a similar pattern.

Settlements modeled after the "protocol of peace" negotiated by Brandeis established the preferential union shop, lowered the workweek to an average of 50 hours, abolished contracting—the source of the "sweating system"—and provided permanent mediation machinery for settling grievances and overseeing working conditions. Both sides assigned officials to boards; under an impartial chairman and his staff of professional mediators, they dealt with every alleged infraction on all levels of the industry.

For men like Schiff and Marshall, class warfare in the Jewish quarter endangered the position of all Jews; to contain radicalism, they expected Jewish bosses to be reasonable. They also linked the labor problem to settling the newcomers; a more rational organization of the industry, therefore, was part of the Jewish community's responsibility to aid the immigrants. Enough Jewish manufacturers were concerned with their standing in the community to make them amenable to compromise. The union leaders—Morris Hillquit (1869–1933), Meyer London (1871–1926), Benjamin Schlesinger (1876–1932), Max Pine (1866–1928), and Sidney Hillman (1887–1946)—were all committed socialists, but they were bread-and-butter trade-union men at the bargaining table. They shared a Yiddish world with their adversaries and readily accepted the Jewish communal leaders as mediators.

The International Ladies Garment Workers Union (ILGWU), organized in 1900, and the Amalgamated Clothing Workers Union (ACWU), organized in 1914, were the main beneficiaries, but the smaller unions, such as the furriers and the hat and cap makers, expanded as well. In 1917, 250,000 Jews and many non-

Jews belonged to these unions. The ILGWU started the first union health center, and its social unionism blossomed into programs of medical care, cooperative housing, unemployment and health insurance, recreational and vacation programs, and retirement benefits. Union economists studied the industry, and union negotiators recommended ways for improving productivity.

Until the New Deal, the union leaders and the rank and file retained much of their European radical heritage derived from the Bund, the Russian Jewish labor movement, many of whose supporters had emigrated after the abortive Russian Revolution of 1905. They considered trade unions as part of a crusade for socialist ideals. Though only a minority were actual members of the Socialist party or the affiliated Jewish Socialist Federation, the Jewish labor movement mobilized impressive support for the party's candidates in New York City elections. In 1914 the Socialist party achieved its greatest election success when Meyer London, a popular labor lawyer, was elected to Congress from the Lower East Side. London told his victory rally that he would show Washington "what the East Side Jew is." Ethnic pride counted for as much as Socialist party principles in his position, and the district elected him twice more before it was gerrymandered out of existence. The party reached its peak in New York in 1917 when Morris Hillquit, a founding father of the Jewish trade-union movement, gained 22 percent of the mayoralty vote, and ten Socialist assemblymen, seven aldermen, and a municipal court judge were elected.

The Yiddish press contributed decisively to the collective identity of Jewish workingmen. The *Jewish Daily Forward* (f. 1897) with a daily circulation that climbed from 54,000 in 1908 to 175,000 a decade later, became the popularizer of radical ideas, the interpreter of the United States to the immigrant, and the forum for Yiddish men of letters. Under its influential editor, Abraham Cahan (1860–1951), the *Forward* served as the informal coordinating body of the movement. It reported union events daily, took strong positions on trade-union policy, and during strikes exhorted the workers and raised funds for the strikers. During the years 1908 to 1918 four other dailies were published: the radical *Warheit,* the Orthodox *Tageblat* and *Morgen Zhurnal,* and the liberal-nationalist *Tog.* A score of weeklies represented all socialist schools of thought.

Ambivalence characterized the relationship between the leaders of the labor movement (less so the rank and file) and the Jewish community. Radical leaders saw the struggle of Russian Jewish workingmen against Russian Jewish garment manufacturers as precluding communal collaboration; as assimilationists they also foresaw the amalgamation of all nationality groups into a "cosmopolitan American nation." Although the claims that Orthodoxy was reactionary became less strident as time passed, they remained part of the movement's European inheritance. Zionists were dangerous dreamers, diverting the attention of the masses from the class struggle to pipe dreams of rebuilding Palestine.

The tactics of the labor movement nevertheless took

for granted a bedrock of ethnic unity. Striking unions appealed to the entire community for aid and good will; the *Forward* was alert to the ethnic sensibilities and interests of its readers. When the community mobilized all its resources to aid European Jewry during World War I, the Jewish labor movement lent its support. Influential intellectuals formulated a doctrine of secular ethnicity grounded in Yiddish culture and appropriate to America's pluralistic society. At the rank and file level, boundaries blurred. Many saw no conflict between remaining loyal to their landsmanshaft, attending synagogue, sending their children to the heder, sympathizing with Zionism, and belonging to a union.

The significance of the Zionist movement far exceeded its numbers; it had only 12,000 members in 1914. Although immigrants constituted most of its membership, it included an influential group of Americanized and native-born Jews. In the decade before World War I, its emphasis became cultural rather than political. American Zionism saw in the modern resettlement of Palestine (which had begun in 1881) a natural habitat for a renaissance of the Hebrew language and culture. The effort to support that undertaking and the effect of the revived center on the Jewish communities of the diaspora would contribute to the survival of Jews everywhere. Since assimilation loomed as the greatest danger, preservation of the Jewish collectivity transcended all particularist conceptions of Judaism, and ethnic survival depended on the cooperation of all factions.

Established middle-class American Jews, well integrated into American life, saw the flood of Russian Jewish immigrants as a threat to their own status and as a burdensome problem. Throughout the 1880s and 1890s, leaders of the Jewish charities begged their European confreres to limit or stop the flow of immigration to the United States or at least exercise a rigorous selection. But organizations like the Alliance Israelite Universelle and the Hilfsverein der Deutschen Juden, which extended aid and eased the journey to the United States, were in no position to control the immigrant tide. As it swelled, American Jews were sensitive to the mounting anti-immigration and anti-Semitic feelings among American Gentiles. Their spokesmen criticized both the religious medievalism of the Orthodox Jews and the dangerous radicalism of the socialists.

After the Civil War, Jews had appeared with greater frequency in popular American literature as sinister and mercenary Shylocks demanding their pound of flesh. In 1862 General Ulysses S. Grant issued an order expelling "Jews as a class" from the Union lines for allegedly trading with the enemy. In the 1880s a pattern of social discrimination excluded upper-class Jews from the elite social clubs that 10 and 20 years before had accepted them. Summer resorts began turning them away, and the phrase "we prefer not to entertain Hebrews" commonly appeared in advertisements. Jacob Schiff, one of the most munificent philanthropists of the time, complained in 1898 of the "tacit understanding" that excluded Jews from the "trustee rooms of Columbia College, of the public museums, the public library, and many similar institutions."

By the end of the century, the stereotype of the Jews had become more specific and virulent; they were the money powers, manipulating international finance and involved in a giant conspiracy to dominate the world. Shylock had become Rothschild. The Boston Brahmin Henry Adams expressed his frustration and anger at his class's loss of place and power when he wrote in the 1890s of "a society of Jews and brokers" in which "I have no place. I detest it [the times], and everything that belongs to it, and live only in the wish to see the end of it, with all its infernal Jewry." Ignatius Donnelly, representing a western agrarian radicalism, published a utopian novel, *Caesar's Column* (1891), about a Jewish plot to take over the world. A bitter and defeated Populist leader, Tom Watson, became viciously anti-Semitic as well as anti-Catholic in his declining years in Georgia politics.

In 1913 a notorious and unprecedented anti-Semitic episode, the Leo Frank case, gained national attention. In April, Frank, a Jewish industrialist raised in Brooklyn, New York, was charged with the murder of a 14-year-old girl employed in the Atlanta, Georgia, factory that he managed. The trial took place amidst a frenzy of anti-Jewish agitation fanned, in particular, by the venomous articles that Tom Watson published in his weekly, *The Jeffersonian*. Frank was convicted on the basis of inconclusive evidence and sentenced to death. His appeals for retrial, which reached the Supreme

Court, were rejected. In June 1915, Governor John Sla-
ton, convinced of Frank's innocence, commuted the
death penalty to life imprisonment. The governor's act
set off a fresh round of anti-Semitic press attacks
against Northern Jews and a wave of economic boy-
cotts and incitement to physical violence against local
Jews. On August 16, 1915, a mob kidnapped Frank
from prison and lynched him.

Racist and anti-Semitic theories imported from Europe—of Joseph Ernest Renan, Joseph Arthur de Go-
bineau, and Houston S. Chamberlain—merged with
nativist notions. According to these views, clannish-
ness, vulgarity, greed, physical inferiority, parasitism,
and intellectualism were inherited traits that the Jews
were incapable of shedding. The identification of the
Russian Jews with the established American Jews as
one racial group confounded and intimidated the
Americanized Jewish community.

Notwithstanding the antipathy of the Americanized
Jews to the Russian immigrants and the social and cultural distance between them, the older settlers accepted
responsibility for the physical welfare and social adjustment of the newcomers. In part their response was
self-serving: expediting the integration of the new arrivals would remove the stigma the immigrants placed
on all of them. However, American Jews also felt com-
passion for victims of oppression and recognized their
common identity. While they complained of the continued flow of immigration, they opened their philanthropic institutions to the Russian Jews, raised funds to

meet their needs, and fought efforts to limit immigration by law.

At first the community simply expanded its facilities and established new ones. Between 1878 and 1890, for example, some 90 new or reorganized YMHAs supplemented their cultural and recreational programs with specific services for young immigrants. Communities began to add vocational training schools, settlement houses, homes for delinquent youths, and agencies for assisting young women and the handicapped. The notions of scientific philanthropy guided the lay leaders and functionaries. The National Conference of Jewish Charities, formed in 1900, stimulated institutional reforms and encouraged clarification of issues and formulation of policy. National agencies were established to deal with family desertion and to divert immigrants to agriculture or to the interior cities.

During these years the first country-wide organization of Jewish women was established. Founded in 1893 at the Columbia Exposition held in Chicago, the National Council of Jewish Women, headed by Hannah G. Solomon (1858–1942), dealt in its early years with problems of philanthropy, education, and religion. However, within a decade of its founding, it developed a broad social, cultural, and vocational program designed to assist single women immigrants and protect them against white slavery.

In response to the rapid expansion of the older charitable societies and the mushrooming of new ones, 23 cities had organized local federations of Jewish charities by 1914. Their immediate purpose was joint fund-raising to increase income, but only institutions with modern standards and nonsectarian policies were eligible for such financing, so the federation tended to exclude the Orthodox institutions and those established by the immigrants. Thus the elite sought to maintain their control over the absorption of the immigrants and reduce to a minimum the detrimental effect of "inferior and alien" influences.

Americanization dominated the thought and the policy of the lay leadership. Jewish settlement houses in New York, Boston, Cleveland, Chicago, Milwaukee, and Cincinnati, such as the Educational Alliance, aimed to be of an "Americanizing, educational, social and humanizing character—for the moral and intellectual improvement of the inhabitants of the East Side." The Alliance offered a rich program in art, music appreciation, drama, physical education, English, civics, and domestic science. In its early years it prohibited the use of Yiddish in public programs, but after 1900 it softened its antipathy to Yiddish culture in an attempt to reach its constituents more effectively. Uptown philanthropists, including Jacob Schiff, Louis Marshall, and Daniel Guggenheim (1856–1930), financed the reorganization of the neo-Orthodox Jewish Theological Seminary (JTS), although they themselves were Reform Jews. To head it, they brought Solomon Schechter (1847–1915), reader in rabbinics at Cambridge University, a traditionalist of eastern European background with impeccable academic credentials. The JTS was to prepare young Russian Jews to be rabbis, faithful to

tradition and at the same time leaders in Americanization. Young American-trained Russian Jews were appointed to administer the institutions of the established community.

A number of factors drew the old and new groups together. The Jewish labor movement and the Russian
Jewish intellectuals won the attention of urban reform-
ers. Brandeis's mediation of the cloak makers' strike in
1910 and his acceptance of the chairmanship of the
board of arbitration renewed this assimilated German
Jew's interest in his people; he became one of their outstanding leaders. American Jewish leaders were also
influenced by the views of settlement workers, whose
criticism of quick Americanization as socially disinte-
grative found wide support, for Jewish survivalists
were at the same time elaborating these attitudes into
theories of ethnic pluralism.

Between 1903 and 1914, crises at home and abroad
interacted to spur communal undertakings on a new
scale. The 1903 Kishinev pogrom and the two years of
violence and bloodshed that followed elicited an unprecedented outburst of activity. Ad hoc committees
and coordinating bodies raised emergency funds for
relief work, organized mass protest meetings, and negotiated with the highest echelons of government to intercede on behalf of Russia's Jews. The experience provoked a public debate over the need for a permanent,
central agency for American Jewry. The immigrant
community demanded a representative body elected
by all Jewish organizations. In response, the German
Jewish elite in 1906 formed the American Jewish Com-

mittee (AJC) to defend Jewish interests. With men of
the stature and means of Schiff, Marshall, Oscar Straus,
Julius Rosenwald, Cyrus Adler (1863–1940), and Julian
W. Mack (1866–1943), the AJC assumed the leadership
of American Jewry on national issues.

The AJC, sensitive to accusations of elitism, coopted
to its councils—though not to its inner circles—Zionists and immigrant leaders and supported an ambitious
program for creating a new communal structure. Under
its aegis, local community councils would coordinate
all Jewish activities in their districts. The one major attempt to organize an all-embracing communal polity,
the New York Kehillah, which was established in 1909,
foundered in internal dissension and apathy a decade
later. In national affairs, the AJC lobbied against immi-
gration-restriction legislation and campaigned to abro-
gate the commercial treaty between Russia and the
United States. Inspired by the need of the German Jewish leaders to reassert their hegemony, the AJC used its
position to defend the rights of the Russian Jews, who,
in return, accepted its leadership, although they re-
sented the imperiousness of the notables and criticized
their assimilationist philosophy.

The rapid Americanization of the second generation
and their alienation from their ethnic heritage occupied
the attention of communal leaders and young intellectuals during these years. Existing philosophies seemed
unlikely to stem the tide of assimilation. Reform Judaism had removed all barriers to Americanization,
and Orthodoxy survived only in the isolated immigrant

synagogues and sterile heders of the Jewish quarter. Survivalists sought a broader interpretation of Judaism that would stress the possibility of creating a viable ethnic culture in America. Israel Friedlaender (1876– 1920), a young professor of Bible at the JTS, and Judah L. Magnes (1877–1948), a Reform rabbi and Zionist, wrote, lectured, and used the small but influential Zionist organization to spread their ideas that Jewish survival depended on a synthesis of "religion plus nationalism." "In the great palace of American civilization," Friedlaender wrote in 1907, "we shall occupy our own corner, which we will decorate and beautify to the best of our taste and ability, and make . . . an object of admiration for all the dwellers of the palace." Those who considered ethnic survival both desirable and compatible with American life rejected the melting-pot concept in favor of ethnic pluralism. In 1909 Magnes delivered a sermon entitled, "A Republic of Nationalities," in which he declared that a multiethnic society would enrich American culture and sustain the psychic health of the nation. Strong roots in one's ethnic heritage would avoid the social disorganization caused by immigration and assure a sound integration into American society.

Horace Kallen (1882–1974), a young professor of philosophy and a Zionist, offered a more secular interpretation. Hebraism, the total historical experience of the Jews, constituted the basis for Jewish survival and was a vital component of American civilization. Kallen's influential essay, "Democracy versus the Melting Pot," argued that ethnic self-realization was a part of democracy. Authentic America was a "democracy of nationalities."

Others elaborated on these theories. In 1915 before a Fourth of July audience in Boston's Faneuil Hall, Brandeis declared that "the new nationalism adopted by America" proclaimed the "right and the duty" of each "race or people" to develop and that such "differentiative development" was to the benefit of the United States. On another occasion Brandeis proclaimed, "To be good Americans, we must be better Jews, and to be better Jews, we must become Zionists."

Critical of the secular-nationalist emphasis and the ethnic separatism implied in the Kallen-Brandeis position, the young Jewish educator Isaac B. Berkson (1891–1975) enlarged upon the Friedlaender-Magnes approach. A protégé of Friedlaender and a staff member of the New York Kehillah's Bureau of Jewish Education, which was directed by Samson Benderly (1876–1944), Berkson presented a "community theory" of American life. He believed that Kallen's "federation of nationalities" assigned too powerful a place to ethnicity, which was inconsonant with the free play of democratic forces. The ethnic group was not self-perpetuating; one had to nurture it within a voluntaristic setting. Its survival depended on the education of the young. The community's ethnic school, which should be supplementary to the public school, was the primary agency of group maintenance.

All these theories of survivalism influenced communal policy. In the decade after 1910 the Friedlaender-Benderly-Berkson view prevailed in the movement to establish a modern Jewish educational system. Around the Kallen-Brandeis approach, with its strong ethnic and democratic motifs, the anti-elitists, anti-assimilationists, and secularists rallied to challenge the established leadership.

During World War I and the immediate postwar period, the attention of the American Jewish community shifted to events overseas. East European Jewry, trapped between the contending armies on the eastern front and then caught in the Russian civil wars, suffered famine, expulsion, and large-scale pogroms. Immigrants, fearful for their kinsmen, funneled aid and personal remittances to the homeland town and family through their societies and institutions. The sense of obligation in the community led to an unprecedented collaborative undertaking to provide relief. American Jewry was very aware of its new role as the one Jewish center of strength and influence unscathed by war. It bore the responsibility for carrying on the struggle for political equality and the right of self-determination.

The creation of the American Jewish Joint Distribution Committee (JDC), the leading agency for overseas relief, expressed this new temper. Although the German Jewish elite supplied the directors and the largest contributors—Felix Warburg (1871–1937), son-in-law of Schiff and senior partner in the firm of Kuhn, Loeb, was chairman—Orthodox and labor relief organizations were constituent members and, despite disputes over policy, the JDC remained united. Between 1914 and 1918 it raised slightly over $16.5 million, and in the first four postwar years, an additional $47.4 million.

A sophisticated and efficient organization gathered and distributed these funds. With extraordinary effectiveness, the JDC fund-raising apparatus reached all sectors of the Jewish population and became a unifying force. The transfer and distribution of aid entailed delicate diplomatic negotiations with the State Department and with governments at war as well as complex political dealings with local groups. By the early 1920s the JDC had established a vast relief network in Europe staffed by field workers and specialists. In addition to direct relief, it also developed programs of economic self-help, health and child care, and community reconstruction. At the height of its work, the JDC was aiding 700,000 Jews.

The cautious AJC, headed by the very able Louis Marshall, had preempted the area of diplomacy and politics. When the Zionists in early 1915 led a movement for a democratically elected central body, an American Jewish Congress, the AJC regarded the movement as a populist challenge to its hegemony and as a menace to the position of Jews in American society. The AJC notables viewed secularism—particularly secular Zionism, with its implied political loyalty to a foreign cause—with apprehension and the congress movement as an attempt to "consolidate the Jews of America into a separate nationalistic group." The leading spokesmen for the congress movement, Brandeis and Stephen S. Wise (1874–1949), a popular young

Reform rabbi, social reformer, and Zionist, condemned the AJC as oligarchic and as misunderstanding American democracy and the Jewish collectivity. The Zionist organization they headed had increased tenfold during these years and had won to its ranks prominent figures like Julian Mack, Felix Frankfurter (1882–1965), Bernard Flexner (1865–1945), and Eugene Meyer (1875–1959). Notably, Hadassah, the women's Zionist Organization founded by Henrietta Szold (1860–1945) in 1912, began its remarkable growth, becoming the Jewish organization with the largest membership.

Thus the immediate political issues became entangled with fundamental questions of the character of Jewish group identity and the nature of American society. The congress issue provoked an ardent debate that engaged all segments of American Jewry. America's entry into the war, the fall of the Russian tsar, and Britain's Balfour Declaration, supporting a Jewish homeland in Palestine, further intensified the conflict over principles and power, though by then a compromise had established a congress whose scope was narrowly defined.

In 1918 delegates representing the whole spectrum of Jewish organizational life, including some reluctant emissaries from the Jewish labor movement, met to select their representatives to the Paris Peace Conference. Those chosen, a cross section of the American Jewish community, were instructed to support demands for Jewish civil and group rights in the new states to be recognized at Versailles and to support the cause of a Jewish home in Palestine. The diplomatic skills of Marshall, the dominant figure of the delegation, enabled him to balance a maze of conflicting views within his own group and among the European Jewish representatives and the Zionists. His lobbying was instrumental in winning guarantees of minority rights for Jews and other ethnic groups in the treaties of the eastern European nations.

The congress convened a second time in 1920 and, as previously agreed, received the delegation's report and disbanded. Those who favored a permanent organization remained to announce the immediate establishment of a new congress under Stephen Wise. It was politically more liberal, activist, and pro-Zionist than the AJC, whose preeminence it challenged, but the congress could no longer claim to speak in the name of all American Jewry.

American Jews found the path to cooperation easy when it came to overseas relief and philanthropy. On issues that touched on ideology, achieving a consensus proved more difficult. More elusive still was the goal of recasting American Jewry into a democratic communal polity. Nevertheless, by 1920 a functional pluralism existed; American Jews had become an interdependent community despite their diversity.

The near-cessation of immigration from 1915 to 1920 coincided with improved economic conditions that markedly raised the standard of living for the mass of Jewish workers. The average annual income of a garment worker in New York City nearly tripled between 1914 and 1919. Workingmen as well as merchants and white-collar workers moved out of the ghettos. The dichotomy between the German Jewish givers and the Russian Jewish receivers belonged to the past. America's entry into the war also contributed to acculturation. About 250,000 Jews served in the armed forces, the majority of them young immigrants. Jewish organizations fostered, and the Yiddish press publicized, citizenship and Americanization programs and civilian war-aid activities. Sensitivity to anti-Semitism and a need to demonstrate the patriotism of the group brought antagonists together in demonstrations of unity in which a newly self-confident Russian Jewish element and second-generation professionals and communal functionaries asserted themselves and were able to challenge or share leadership with the elite.

IMMIGRATION FROM 1924 TO THE END OF WORLD WAR II

In 1921 nearly 120,000 Jewish immigrants entered the United States, most of them joining families that had arrived earlier. After the passage of the Immigration Restriction Act of 1924, Jewish immigration fell to 10,000; thereafter new immigrants assumed a marginal place in American Jewish life, and rapid acculturation shaped the society.

Occupational change was a critical component. Within the span of one or two generations, eastern European Jews transformed themselves from a working-class population to a middle-class group in business, white-collar jobs, and the professions. In 1900, 60 percent of the gainfully employed immigrant men were in industry. In the 1930s (according to data from a cluster of smaller cities and from Pittsburgh), the proportion had shrunk to 16.7 percent in the smaller cities and 24.2 percent in Pittsburgh. The proportion in industry of the general work force was two to three times that. In 1900 about 25 percent of the immigrant Jews were in trade or held clerical positions. By the 1930s the proportion had grown to 57 percent in the smaller cities and 63 percent in Pittsburgh, twice that of the general work force. In 1900 about 3 percent of the Russian Jews were in the professions; three decades later, Jewish professionals accounted for about 17 percent and 13 percent in the two surveys, significantly higher than the proportion for the general population. New York, because of its large Jewish population, higher ratio of immigrants, and the dominance of the garment trades, always had a higher proportion of Jews in industry. In the 1930s about 35 percent were in manufacturing, 34 percent in trade, and 11 percent in the professions.

A study comparing foreign- and native-born Jews in three localities during these years sheds some light on the mobility pattern of the second generation. Ten percent of the native-born compared to 18 percent of the foreign-born were in industry; 53 percent of the native-born compared to 62 percent of the foreign-born were in trade. In the professions the figures were 19 percent and 7 percent. In Boston "by 1930, the East European Jews were sufficiently established to give their sons as large a head start as the German Jews had in the late 19th century . . . The rate of initial white-collar job-holding" for Russian Jewish sons in 1930 was 71 percent; for German Jewish sons in the late 1890s it had been 73 percent.

Eastern European Jews became leaders in the motion-picture industry. Beginning as owners of storefront movie theaters in the immigrant neighborhoods (at a time when silent films offered no language barrier), they branched out into film distribution, chains of movie theaters, and then production itself. By the 1930s all but one of the major companies were managed and owned by Jews: Jesse Lasky, Adolph Zukor, and Barney Balaban (Paramount), Carl Laemmle (Universal), Samuel Goldfish (Goldwyn), Louis B. Mayer and Marcus Loew (Metro-Goldwyn-Mayer), Jack and Harry Cohn (Columbia), Sol Brill and William Fox (Twentieth-Century-Fox), Al Lichtman (United Artists) and Sam, Jack, Albert, and Harry Warner (Warner Brothers). Kuhn, Loeb and Company was the first bank to finance motion pictures. The men who entered the industry when it was still unstructured and financially risky shaped a powerful vehicle of mass culture.

The main route out of the working class remained trade. Jews became proprietors, salesmen, and providers of commercial services or white-collar workers such as bookkeepers and clerks. A professional career was a more difficult path and more accessible for the second generation. Professional status was highly esteemed by the group, and the material rewards and self-employment it promised were weighty considerations. Being a scholar carried great prestige in a culture that so revered learning. For immigrant parents, the discipline of learning was a social imperative they well understood, and the utilitarian nature of education in the United States reinforced it. They encouraged their children to remain in school and go to college. The physicians, dentists, lawyers, and pharmacists serving the immigrant quarter confirmed the promised rewards.

Although accounting and pharmacy were popular, the number of Jews in medicine, dentistry, and law was even more notable. In New York City in 1937, Jews made up 25 percent of the population but 65 percent of its lawyers and judges, 64 percent of its dentists, and 55 percent of its physicians. In Cleveland in 1938, Jews constituted 7.7 percent of the population, 23 percent of the lawyers, 21 percent of the physicians, and 18 percent of the dentists.

The middle-class character of American Jews was also manifest during the 1920s and 1930s in their lowered birthrate. In the first two decades of the century, Jewish and Italian immigrant families were about the same size. By 1925 the Jews of New York showed a lower birthrate than the rest of the population, and it declined even further in the 1930s. Between 1920 and 1940, the decline was double that of the birthrate for the native white population as a whole.

In the interwar years the regional distribution of the Jewish population changed very little. The five cities that accounted for 63 percent of the Jewish population in 1918 maintained the same rank order 20 years later. Among the five cities that accounted for the next 9 percent, rank-order changes were minor. Los Angeles entered the list in the 1930s at seventh place.

Migration within the city accelerated, as the lower-middle-class and middle-class neighborhoods absorbed the young and newly prosperous. The older, poorer, and more religious Jews were left behind. In Harlem the rise and fall of the Jewish community was complete by 1930. Of 177,000 Jews living there in 1923, fewer than 5,000 remained in 1930. More commonly, however, neighborhoods that began receiving substantial numbers of Jews before World War I expanded rapidly during the war and the decade that followed, then remained stable until after World War II, restrained by the Depression and the war years.

In many of the new neighborhoods, the Jewish population was no less concentrated than in the ghettos it had left behind. Discriminatory housing practices and prejudice explain this in part, but the desire to remain in a Jewish environment was also important. By the end of the 1920s, a social hierarchy of neighborhoods reached to the suburbs, where the most acculturated and affluent of the Russian Jews were closing the gap with the old German Jewish families. In 1930 half the members of the Reform temples were of eastern European origin, and the most successful of the Americanized Russian Jews were elected as officers in philanthropic organizations and as members of the German Jewish clubs. A substantial segment of them were still Yiddish-speaking, however. Nearly half the Jewish population in 1920 declared Yiddish to be its mother tongue. In 1940 the proportion was somewhat more than a third. Even outside the ghetto they continued to be consumers of a flourishing Yiddish culture. In the mid-twenties, five Yiddish dailies were published in New York City and five more outside it.

Two institutions were found in almost every middle-class Jewish community; synagogues and community centers or YMHAs met traditional needs, represented group continuity, and satisfied social and recreational interests in a congenial setting.

In the 1920s over 1,000 synagogues were established in the new neighborhoods. Nearly all were sizable; some were elaborate structures with classrooms and recreational facilities. The old-town or regional organizing principle of the immigrant congregation had disappeared. Though many of the synagogues were Orthodox, they were meant to appeal to a modern, middle-class, Americanized public in a changed neighborhood. They overlooked the heterodoxy of many of their congregants and tried to win the indifferent back to Orthodoxy. They established schools to attract young families to the congregation and engaged "modern," English-speaking rabbis. The effort to revitalize American Orthodoxy included the founding of Yeshiva College in 1928 under the presidency of Bernard Revel (1865–1941). The goal of the college, which was linked to the Isaac Elchanan Theological Seminary, Orthodoxy's largest rabbinical school, was to educate lay as well as professional leaders.

Conservative Judaism also found a new following. With intellectual roots in 19th-century western Europe and the United States, the movement stressed "the maintenance of Jewish tradition in its historical continuity" but countenanced change in religious practice, provided it was done with reverence for "historical Judaism." Solomon Schechter, the president of the JTS from 1902 to his death in 1915, gave form and direction to this Conservative style, carefully eschewing doctrinal formulations. By the 1920s graduates of the JTS were entering the rabbinate, and the JTS was a prestigious center of Jewish scholarship. Schechter created a formal body, the United Synagogues of America, as an institutional framework. For Americanized Russian Jews and their offspring, elements of tradition coupled with innovations of convenience satisfied their desire for continuity and for accommodation to American middle-class norms. The Conservative synagogues were also centers for a great many civic, social, and cultural functions. By the end of World War II it had become the largest wing of Judaism.

The Jewish community center was a secular institution from the outset, Jewish but nonsectarian. An outgrowth of the YMHAs of the 19th century and the Jewish-sponsored settlement houses of the early 20th, it blended the two purposes of its predecessors: to give young Americanized Jews a place to pursue their essentially American interests and to hasten the Americanization of the immigrants. In the 1920s, when these centers were moved to the new neighborhoods, they continued to be supported by the federations, whose sponsorship was justified on the grounds that the second generation needed guidance and a suitable setting as they took their place in American society. Professionals, increasingly influential in the management of the centers, supplied the theory: character building and self-development through recreational programs and social group work—by definition nonsectarian—would imbue the young with democratic and humanistic values. The 300 centers, with nearly 400,000 members by the late 1930s, remained, ideologically at least, the domain of the nonsectarians. Financed by the Jewish community, staffed by Jewish volunteers and professionals, and serving a Jewish public at a time when social discrimination outside the neighborhood was common, the centers were an ethnic haven.

Synagogues and community centers reflected only in part the state of the American Jewish community. Only a third of the Jewish families in 1930 were affiliated with a synagogue, and only a quarter of the Jewish children attended religious schools. Many were satisfied with a superficial or peripheral identification with the community. For a considerable number, residing in a Jewish neighborhood was the sole manifestation of ethnic identity.

Mordecai M. Kaplan, a religious thinker associated with the Conservatives, was a founder of the Reconstructionist movement and influential in the JTS. His ideas found expression in his book *Judaism as a Civilization* (1934), in which he offered an overarching framework for the diversity and secularization of Jewish life. His theological formulations raised a storm of opposition among Conservative and Orthodox rabbis. Judaism, he wrote, embraced "language, folkways, patterns of social organization, social habits and standards, spiritual ideals, which give individuality to a people and differentiate it from other peoples." Jewish religion was the expression of group consciousness. Kaplan accorded a central place to Palestine in his program and called for an all-encompassing reconstruction of Jewish life and Jewish communal organization, although he acknowledged the priority that American life had on the individual's loyalty. The majority of American Jews agreed with Kaplan but were not prepared to make the commitments he felt were necessary to improve the quality and the efficacy of the community's institutions. Religiously skeptical or apathetic, they sought a Jewish identity that would be compatible with their Americanness and their liberal secular outlook.

The frenzied nativism of the 1920s intensified anti-Jewish agitation. The anti-Semitism that had taken shape the decade before made the Jews particularly vulnerable to the xenophobia of the times. During the Red Scare, the idea of the Jew as Bolshevik plotting to overthrow the state led government agents and journalists to search for revolutionaries among the Jewish radical movements. At congressional and legislative hearings, at public meetings, and in the organs of the Ku Klux Klan, immigrant Jews were portrayed as architects of the Russian Revolution and as agents of world Communism preparing to seize control of America. In 1920 Henry Ford added his powerful voice to the anti-Semitic campaign in his *Dearborn Independent*, a weekly he distributed through his thousands of dealerships, featuring accounts of cabals of Jewish bankers maneuvering to gain control of the economy. Especially pernicious was the wide publicity it gave to the notorious anti-Semitic tract, *The Protocols of the Elders of Zion*, which purported to be the report of a secret Jewish plan to establish a world dictatorship through financial machinations, war, and revolution.

The debate over immigration restriction from 1918 to 1924 provided a public platform for nativist racist theories. The notion of Nordic superiority, which became the justification for the national-origins quotas of the 1924 immigration law, was laced with anti-Jewish animus. One influential State Department report described the Jewish immigrants in transit to the United States as "of the usual ghetto type . . . filthy, un-American and often dangerous in their habits . . . abnormally twisted, [their] dullness and stultification resulting from past years of oppression and abuse."

Although virulent anti-Semitism diminished in the mid-1920s, the prewar pattern of social discrimination continued. The barriers that affluent German Jews had met in seeking entrée to the elite clubs and resorts and, for their children, to the prestigious schools had widened to restrain the more modest ambitions of upwardly mobile Russian Jews. Housing restrictions in new areas of settlement and job discrimination in white-collar employment were common after 1910. A decade later the movement to the better neighborhoods encountered a well-developed system of restrictive real-estate covenants. The second generation met harsher barriers in the job market. Newspaper employment advertisements showed a sharp rise in discriminatory restrictions against Jews between 1920 and 1926, followed by a modest decline and then a renewed rise in the 1930s. Jewish stenographers, bookkeepers, and sales help found the large corporations and chain stores closed to them. Outside the large cities, Jews and Catholics rarely found employment in the public schools.

Discrimination in higher education particularly agitated the Jewish community. In the early 1920s the eastern universities, with large numbers of Jewish students, imposed quotas, which they defended as a means of correcting geographic and social imbalance of the student body or as a prophylactic measure against growing anti-Semitism. When Harvard's president, Lawrence Lowell, recommended a formal quota for the latter reason, Jewish leaders protested vigorously: "The only tests that we can recognize [for admission]," the AJC's Louis Marshall wrote, "are those of character and scholarship." The student body supported Lowell, but in the end the faculty defeated the proposal. Medical schools were most severe in their restrictive policies. The number of Jewish students enrolled in New York State medical schools dropped from 214 in 1920 to 108 in 1940. Marshall's dictum did not become university policy generally until after World War II.

Within the academic community, discrimination was reflected in rare faculty appointment of Jews and in their exclusion from fraternities. Ludwig Lewisohn (1882–1955), already a man of literary attainments when he completed his graduate studies, nevertheless found all academic doors closed. Lionel Trilling (1905–1975), who began teaching literature at Columbia University in 1931, was the first Jew appointed to the English department. Thurman Arnold (1891–1969) of the

Yale Law School, trying to place one of his graduates (Abe Fortas, 1910–, a future justice of the Supreme Court) in the mid-1930s, received a reply from the dean at Northwestern University that his colleagues had not once appointed a Jewish candidate during his tenure at the school. Another indication of social discrimination on the campuses was the rise in Jewish Greek-letter fraternities: 4 in 1908, 25 in 1926, and 37 ten years later.

In the 1920s personal and communal achievements in some measure offset distress over discrimination, but on both counts, the situation deteriorated in the 1930s. Hitler's accession to power, Nazi expansionism, and anti-Semitism at home struck a population already suffering from the debilitating effects of the Depression. The confluence of economic distress and anti-Semitism provided a fertile field for demagogues preaching hate, while inadequate financial resources and discord among the Jewish community agencies over strategies for counteracting anti-Jewish attitudes impaired their ability to respond.

The German-American Bund represented a direct connection between Nazi Germany and rising domestic anti-Semitism; the bund received funds, organizational leadership, and propaganda material from the German government. Of greater concern was the influence of Charles E. Coughlin, a Roman Catholic priest whose nationwide broadcasts and newspaper, *Social Justice*, won an immense following. His anti-Communist crusade and his populist rhetoric relied on the old stereotypes of the Jews as Communist plotters and international bankers. By 1938 he was justifying the Nazi persecution of Jews as a defense against Communism. Important Catholic diocesan papers supported Coughlin's position and encouraged the Christian Front, an organization propagating anti-Semitism. Between 1939 and 1941, when the United States entered the war, some isolationists attacked the Jews as "the most dangerous force pushing the nation into war" and were echoed in Congress by Senators Burton K. Wheeler and Gerald Nye. During the war public opinion polls showed hostility toward the Jews rising substantially; soon after the war it disappeared almost entirely.

The refugees from Nazi Germany who began arriving in the middle 1930s—from 1935 through 1941 nearly 150,000 came—were for the most part middle-aged and middle-class: 74 percent were over 40; nearly 20 percent were professionals, another 60 percent were in commerce. Manhattan's West Side and Washington Heights, where about half the newcomers settled, became known as the "Fourth Reich." Chicago and San Francisco also had identifiable colonies. Arriving in the middle of the Depression, the refugees at first found it difficult to use their professional and entrepreneurial skills. For this highly educated, cosmopolitan group, cultural isolation and the loss of social and economic status made adjustment particularly painful. In 1941 a study was made to refute charges that the refugees were a burden on the economy; it reported that refugees had established 239 businesses in 82 cities and had created jobs for others.

Albert Einstein (1879–1955), the Nobel laureate in physics, was the best known of a brilliant army of refugee scientists, writers, artists, and scholars. Others like Otto Stern (1888–1969), Leo Szilard (1898–1964), Eugene P. Wigner (1902–), Emilio G. Segrè (1905–), Edward Teller (1908–), and Victor F. Weisskopf (1908–) contributed to atomic research. Psychoanalysis, a field in which Jews had played a dominant role in Europe, was enriched in the United States by outstanding refugees, including Helene Deutsch (1884–1973), Ernst Simmel (1882–1947), Heinz Hartmann (1894–1970), Hanns Sachs (1881–1947), Erich Fromm (1900–), Bruno Bettelheim (1903–), and Erik Erikson (1902–). Among the refugee social scientists were Hannah Arendt (1906–1975), Paul Lazarsfeld (1901–1976), Kurt Lewin (1890–1947), Herbert Marcuse (1898–1979), and Leo Strauss (1899–1973).

All efforts to ease the rigid immigration laws and increase the number of Jewish refugees failed. A bill that would have allowed 20,000 German Jewish children to enter the United States outside the quota was defeated in 1941. Other bills and appeals to the administration to permit refugees to enter by mortgaging future quotas and to open Alaska to them met the same fate. The State Department imposed even more complicated and time-consuming procedures on applications for visas. In mid-1940, when precious unused visas would have saved lives, the official in charge recommended putting "every obstacle in the way" and suggested various administrative devices that would "postpone and postpone and postpone the granting of visas." As reports from Europe described Nazi excesses against the Jews, American Zionists appealed to the administration to pressure Britain to alter its Palestine policy, but no action was taken. Jewish Palestine had been the most important haven for refugees during the 1930s, but Britain drastically reduced immigration in 1939 and deported Jews fleeing Europe who succeeded in reaching its shores. In late 1942 the State Department deliberately suppressed for months the first authoritative underground reports on the Nazi plan to systematically exterminate all Jews.

American Jewry was ill prepared to face the crisis. A conglomeration of institutions and agencies, reflecting different religious persuasions, conceptions of Jewish group life, and strategies of action, frequently competed with or duplicated each other's work. About 25 major organizations with national constituencies were in the field in the 1930s; representatives of 85 national organizations attended the American Jewish Conference in 1943. No less than four central agencies combated anti-Semitism and discrimination. The AJC, the oldest and most prestigious of them, had amassed an impressive record over the years by firmly but unobtrusively interceding in every serious instance of prejudice. It monitored state-church relations, cultivated ties with liberal church and civil-rights groups, litigated cases, and maintained relations with political and government figures. Its image continued to be one of conservative, moderate old German Jewish wealth. In keeping with this elitist cast, it eschewed public action, which it considered undignified and provocative. In the 1930s it clashed with the American Jewish Congress, which regarded itself as representing the mass of

American Jews. Under Stephen Wise's aggressive leadership, the Congress organized demonstrations, boycotted German-made goods, and pursued the type of diplomatic activity that the AJC had considered its sphere. The Anti-Defamation League (ADL) of B'nai B'rith, established in 1913, and the Jewish Labor Committee, established in 1933 to represent the still substantial Jewish trade unions and the Jewish socialists, overlapped in their functions, but they were so genuinely different in outlook that any attempt at coordination or amalgamation was futile.

Raising funds for relief constituted the main collaborative effort, but even there the Zionists and non-Zionists could not agree. Nevertheless, between 1939 and 1945, the JDC sent close to $80 million to Europe, funneling funds when possible to Jewish groups in Nazi-occupied Europe and financing underground escape efforts.

In 1943 the American Jewish Conference attempted to establish a representative body to direct political and rescue efforts, but again, unity was not complete. The conference was able to agree on a program, except on the issue of a declaration in support of a Jewish commonwealth to be established in Palestine at the end of the war. Over that question the Jewish Labor Committee and the AJC withdrew; a Zionist state ran counter to ideological positions long held by the labor committee, and the AJC regarded a sovereign Jewish state as fraught with danger for American Jews because of the specter of dual allegiance.

Thus, at a time when the intervention of the United

States might have saved some from annihilation, the American Jewish community was unable to overcome internal differences and speak with a single voice. Some Jews feared that special pleading for Europe's Jews and for opening Palestine to refugees would make the war a Jewish war. The government viewed rescue efforts as a distraction from prosecution of the war and fended off Jewish pressure for action. The War Department rejected urgent requests in the summer of 1944 to bomb the gas chambers and crematoria at Auschwitz, though the U.S. Air Force was regularly bombing the area. To do so, it was argued, would divert military resources to nonmilitary objectives and extend the war. The dilemma was most poignant for those Jews with influence and with close ties to the Jewish community. Samuel I. Rosenman (1896–1973), Henry Morgenthau, Jr. (1891–1967), Benjamin V. Cohen, and Felix Frankfurter were among Roosevelt's trusted advisers, and Jews had supported Roosevelt and the Democratic party since 1932. Nonetheless Roosevelt did not take any action until 1944, when he created the War Refugee Board to seek ways to rescue Jews. In its brief tenure it showed the feasibility of such activity, but the main priority remained the defeat of the Axis powers.

About 550,000 Jews served in the armed forces. The shared struggle and sacrifices led to a firmer, more certain integration into American society, while the destruction of a third of world Jewry in the Nazi holocaust created a greater sense of group identity. Jews were thereafter both more at home in America and more aware of their ties to Jews in the rest of the world.

1945 TO THE PRESENT

Jews prospered in the postwar years. Those in commerce and the professions profited particularly from an expanding economy, with its rising demand for consumer goods and services. All Jews benefited from the decline in racial and religious discrimination and the resulting expansion of educational and occupational opportunities. The generation that came of age during those years was in the forefront of the civil-rights movement and in liberal and radical politics and was influential in the intellectual life of the country. Though relative newcomers, American Jewry compared with white Protestant society in educational attainments, income, and lifestyle. Largely native-born of Russian Jewish parentage in 1945, the population was third- and fourth-generation American by the 1970s. Although a high level of acculturation characterized a majority of its members, the organized community nevertheless maintained its stability and cohesion.

In the 40 years between 1937 and 1977, the population of the United States increased by over two-thirds, but American Jewry grew by only a fifth, so that the Jewish portion of the population decreased from a high of 3.7 percent in 1937 to 2.7 percent in 1977. The drastic drop in birthrate was arrested momentarily in the 1950s, but it remained among the lowest of all ethnic or religious groups. During these years immigration, though of qualitative importance, was too limited to have much effect on Jewish population growth.

Jews in the United States were also dispersed more widely across the nation in the 1970s (see Table 2). Los Angeles and Miami rose in the ranks of most populous Jewish communities, while Chicago, Cleveland, and Detroit fell. No less typically, Jews joined the flight of the white middle class from the city. By the late 1950s the urban Jewish neighborhoods of the interwar years had been abandoned except for pockets of mostly elderly and impoverished Jews. The rest settled in a ring of suburban settlements, often as distant from one another as from the city. Within these suburban belts, however, they continued to cluster together.

In New York some of the older neighborhoods showed considerable stability, reflecting the persistence of a Jewish working class, strong communal institutions, usually staunchly Orthodox, a concentration of postwar immigrants, and the elderly poor. A 1973 study classified 15 percent of the city's Jews as at or near the poverty level, two-thirds of them over the age of 60. The exodus from the Bronx (538,000 Jews in 1940 to 143,000 in 1977) and parts of Brooklyn (857,000 Jews in 1940 to 514,000 in 1977) showed that New York Jews followed the general Jewish pattern, but at a slower rate and in a more selective fashion. Jewish poor could also be found in the old immigrant neighborhoods of Chicago, Philadelphia, Los Angeles, and Miami. One estimate placed the number at between 400,000 and 800,000, again mostly people aged 65 or over. Too poor to move, clinging to a small business or the comfort of an Orthodox synagogue, they have been frequent victims of crime, failing health, and isolation.

Table 2. Jewish population of selected cities,[a] 1948 and 1977

	1948		1977	
	Number	Percentage of total Jewish population	Number	Percentage of total Jewish population
New York	2,000,000	40.0	New York	1,998,000	34.6
Chicago	300,000	6.0	Los Angeles	455,000	7.9
Philadelphia	245,000	4.9	Philadelphia	350,000	6.0
Los Angeles	225,000	4.5	Chicago	253,000	4.4
Boston	137,345	2.7	Miami	225,000	3.9
Detroit	90,000	1.8	Boston	170,000	2.9
Cleveland	80,000	1.6	Washington, D.C.	120,000	2.0
Baltimore	75,000	1.5	Bergen County, N.J.	100,000	1.7
Newark	56,800	1.1	Essex County, N.J.	95,000	1.6
Pittsburgh	54,000	1.8	Baltimore	92,000	1.6
Total	3,263,145	65.9		3,858,000	66.6

Source: *American Jewish Yearbook* 51(1950): 71–73; 77(1977): 275–278, 318; 78(1978): 254–260.
a. Includes contiguous suburban areas; Bergen County includes Englewood; Essex County includes Newark.

Prosperity, combined with the removal of educational and social barriers, opened up opportunities for the Jews of the postwar generation. Supported by the achievements of their parents, many of whom were independent businessmen, they entered the professions or, as white-collar workers, looked forward to becoming managers and executives. In 1971, 40 percent of a sample work force were employed as managers or administrators, a proportion three or four times that of the general population, and 29 percent of men and 24 percent of women were professionals. In 1963, 19 percent of the 45-to-64 age group in Detroit were professionals, compared to 42 percent of the 20-to-34 year age group. By the 1970s over 80 percent of college-age Jews were actually attending college, and 71 percent of all Jews between the ages of 25 and 29 had college degrees.

The numbers of Jewish workers in the clothing industry declined, but they remained heavily represented in management. Jewish businessmen were involved in real estate and in the construction of buildings and shopping centers connected with the move to the suburbs. They were prominent in communications: William Paley (1901–) of CBS and David Sarnoff (1891–1971) of NBC, pioneers of radio in the 1920s and 1930s, guided their networks into the television era; Leonard H. Goldenson (1905–) became president of ABC in the 1960s. The publishing houses of Alfred A. Knopf, Random House, and Simon and Schuster were all owned by Jews.

Jews were heavily represented in entertainment as entrepreneurs and artists, beginning in the 1920s.

Florenz Ziegfeld, Lee Strasberg, and the Schubert brothers were prominent directors and producers. Composers for the musical theater were Irving Berlin, Jerome Kern, George Gershwin, and Richard Rodgers. The list of Jewish entertainers includes Fanny Brice, Eddie Cantor, Al Jolson, Groucho, Harpo, and Zeppo Marx, Milton Berle, Danny Kaye, and Zero Mostel. Conductor-composer Leonard Bernstein and dramatist Arthur Miller were influential figures in the postwar period.

Though the professions that traditionally attracted Jews continued to do so, an enormous number also entered the academic world. The new prestige given scholarly pursuits and scientific research in the United States after the war provided new opportunities in the expanding universities and research institutes of the country. The still-potent, traditional reverence for the intellectual and the promises of greater rewards attracted young Jews to the universities. By 1970 over 10 percent of American professors were Jewish, and in the most prestigious universities the proportion reached 30 percent. Politically they were often liberal or radical, and their religious or ethnic ties were weaker than those of their fellow professors.

Intellectualism, radicalism, and assimilationism produced a number of creative writers, literary critics, and social commentators of Jewish origin. Though they addressed a general public, their work had common attributes that stemmed from their American Jewish milieu. Thoroughly acculturated and economically secure, they sympathized little with their parents' striving for middle-class respectability and the remnants of ethnic heritage. Nobel laureate Saul Bellow (1915–), Bernard Malamud (1914–), and Philip Roth (1933–) scorned the materialism and sterile ethnicity of their elders but also found American society wanting. The critical acclaim these writers received reflected the discontent shared by intellectuals in general. The themes of alienation and the anti-hero were depicted through Jewish characters and circumstances, but they struck a universal chord. These works also introduced the reader to a highly subjective depiction of the American Jewish subculture.

Other American Jewish novelists of distinction included J. D. Salinger, Herbert Gold, Wallace Markfeld, Isaac Rosenfeld, Joseph Heller, and Bruce Jay Friedman. Elie Wiesel's works on the holocaust and Nobel laureate Isaac Bashevis Singer's tales of eastern European Jewish life, translated from the Yiddish, recreated a vanished Jewish world. Among the poets of importance were Delmore Schwartz, Howard Nemerov, Karl Shapiro, and Babette Deutsch. Popular best sellers often dealt with Jewish themes, including Herman Wouk, *Marjorie Morningstar* (1955), Leon Uris, *Exodus* (1958), Chaim Potok, *The Chosen* (1967), and Gerald Green, *The Holocaust* (1978). Philip Rahv, Lionel Trilling, Alfred Kazin, Irving Howe, Susan Sontag, Leslie Fiedler, Irving Kristol, Norman Podhoretz, and Theodore Solotaroff dealt with literature in a broad social and cultural context and became social commentators for journals like *Partisan Review, Dissent, New York Review of Books, New American Review,* and *Commen-*

tary. The proclivity of Jews for sociology drew upon reformist and radical traditions; psychiatry, the most humanistic medical field, continued to attract many.

The reformist-radical zeal that characterized the authentic political tradition of American Jews had its roots both in the Jewish immigrant settlements and in the *noblesse oblige* of the affluent German Jews. Democratic politicians early learned to take into account the issue-oriented Jewish immigrant voter. Al Smith (1873–1944), Tammany's most successful East Side politician, was elected governor with the support and influence of such Jewish liberals as Belle Moskowitz (1877–1933) and Joseph Proskauer (1877–1971). Louis Brandeis, Stephen Wise, and Henry Morgenthau (1856–1946), in their support of Woodrow Wilson, similarly represented the progressive commitment of the established Jews. Politicians who fought immigration restrictions such as Democrat James M. Curley of Boston received overwhelming support from the Jewish voters, and for two decades Tammany elected Henry F. Goldfogle (1856–1929) to the U.S. Congress from the Lower East Side. Republican Theodore Roosevelt's public criticism of anti-Jewish policy in Russia, his appointment of Oscar Straus as the first Jewish cabinet officer, and his praise of Jewish citizens made him a Jewish folk hero.

The reformist tradition of left-of-center liberalism appeared in full form in Jewish support of the New Deal. Unlike others in the New Deal coalition, Jews tended to be equally liberal on political, social, and economic issues. In 1944 Roosevelt's popularity dwindled among many interest groups, but the pro-Roosevelt Jewish vote climbed to over 90 percent. This commitment to a comprehensive liberalism remained strong despite some erosion. In 1952 Democrat Adlai Stevenson received 44 percent of the popular vote but 75 percent of the Jewish vote when he ran for president against Dwight D. Eisenhower. Twenty years later Democrat George McGovern received only 38 percent of the popular vote but 60 to 70 percent of the Jewish vote. Other ethnic and religious groups became more conservative in their political outlook as they grew prosperous, but the Jews retained their essentially New Deal liberal views: legislation on behalf of underprivileged groups, defense of civil liberties and civil rights, and an internationalist foreign policy.

The radical tradition operated in tandem with Jewish liberalism and occasionally merged with it. The Jewish labor movement was involved in radical politics throughout the 1920s and was one of the largest contingents in the Socialist party, though its energy was dissipated in disputes over the unsuccessful efforts of Jewish Communists to dominate the garment workers' unions. Perhaps 15 percent of Communist party members during the 1920s were of Jewish origin. In the thirties, the Soviet Union appeared to some younger radicals to be the single power that was unequivocally opposed to Nazism and Fascism, and Communism seemed the only alternative to continued depression. Popular-front Communism attracted teachers, social workers, and intellectuals.

The New Deal provided an outlet for the political energies of the Jewish labor movement. Trade-union leaders Sidney Hillman and David Dubinsky (1892–), supported by Abe Cahan's socialist *Forward*, turned many away from immigrant radicalism toward Democratic party reform and provided Jewish liberalism with much of its earnestness and constancy. Liberal politics also provided an avenue into public life for those looking beyond the bounds of their ethnic group. Jews have been mainstays of the American Civil Liberties Union (ACLU) and the National Association for the Advancement of Colored People (NAACP) since their inception. The NAACP had two Jewish presidents: Joel E. Spingarn (1875–1939) from 1930 to 1939 and his brother, Arthur B. Spingarn (1878–1971), from 1940 to 1966. Felix Frankfurter, Louis Marshall, Samuel Leibowitz (1893–1978), and Jack Greenberg (1924–) are among the prominent Jewish lawyers who have fought major legal battles on behalf of civil liberties and equal rights. The AJC, the ADL, and the American Jewish Congress early broadened their concerns from anti-Semitism to discrimination in general and to civil rights and church-state questions. During the 1960s the large proportion of Jewish students in anti-Vietnam war activities, protest movements, and such New Left organizations as Students for a Democratic Society showed that the propensity for radical causes carried over to the third and fourth generation.

In the demonstrations, marches, sit-ins, and voter registration campaigns of the 1960s, Jewish students, professors, and rabbis were especially prominent. With the passage of the Civil Rights Acts of 1964 and

1965, American Jews acclaimed what appeared to be the attainment of equal rights for all. The dramatic change in black goals in the mid-sixties, however, generated hostility between the blacks and Jewish liberals, as blacks demanded compensatory measures to close the social and economic gap between themselves and whites. Their rhetoric affronted Jewish sensibilities, and their aggressive tactics, particularly the anti-Semitic slogans of extremists and the denunciations of Israel as racist and imperialist, collided with Jewish interests. Jewish merchants and landlords who had remained in or owned property in black, previously Jewish neighborhoods were victims of violence and vandalism. Jewish civil servants, social workers, and teachers felt threatened by black demands for community control and proportional representation in government service. In the Ocean Hill–Brownsville school district of New York in 1968 the traditional liberal notions of merit, union rights, and nondiscriminatory practices clashed head on with black demands.

Throughout the 1970s "affirmative action"—government enforcement of preferential treatment in hiring, promotion, and college admissions—became an issue of great concern to American Jews. Jewish organizations pressed hard for equality of opportunity but opposed quotas based on race and ethnicity, regarding government recognition of racial and ethnic categories as a dangerously retrogressive step. The same Jewish organizations that had submitted arguments for school desegregation in *Brown* v. *Board of Education* in 1954 and had fought for civil-rights legislation supported

Allen Bakke's challenge to imposed quotas in university admissions, adjudicated by the Supreme Court in 1978.

In the 1960s and 1970s Jewish communal leaders began to fear that social integration was leading to complete assimilation and loss of Jewish identity. The response by those committed to group survival was to adapt older forms and to develop new strategies that would be more congruent with American life.

In the postwar years Jewish Americans were most likely to define themselves in terms of a religious community, and the synagogue gained in prestige and authority. The earlier Jewish ideological movements, specialized service organizations, Yiddish cultural milieu, and compact Jewish neighborhoods with their informal associational networks had provided secular alternatives to the synagogue. The decline of these alternatives coincided with a new religious emphasis that classified Jews as a religious denomination. Will Herberg (1902–1977), who had himself made the intellectual journey from Marxist theoretician to Jewish theologian, called Judaism one of "the three great religious communities." Protestant, Catholic, Jew constituted the three basic subdivisions of the American people, a view that dovetailed with a number of other developments: a religious revival that stimulated church and synagogue attendance, the interfaith movement that emphasized the Judeo-Christian tradition, and a search for consensus and tranquility.

The synagogue became the primary communal institution in the new suburban settlements, modeled on the synagogue center of the 1920s, but enlarged to meet more varied social and cultural requirements. The supplementary religious school was absorbed into the synagogue, and membership in the congregation was the prerequisite for attending it. Transmitting Jewish identity to the young was the principal inducement for joining and supporting the synagogue; it assumed greater importance as the guarantor of ethnic continuity than it had as a house of worship. Few attended services regularly—about 15 percent in one poll—but nearly 50 percent of the Jewish population were members of a synagogue, and many more had been members at some previous time. The smaller the community, the higher the proportion of congregational membership.

Rabbis, educators, cantors, and administrators trained in the central institutions of the various religious wings of Judaism were the bearers of the cultural heritage. Jewish learning among laymen was common only in the most Orthodox synagogues. Vastly expanded theological seminaries, rabbinical associations, federations of congregations, and auxiliary agencies supported the scholarly endeavors, research, and professional training in those institutions, which served as resources for the transmission of the religious and cultural heritage. The influence of religious thinkers, such as Mordecai Kaplan, Louis Finkelstein (1895–), chancellor of the JTS, Abraham J. Heschel (1907–1972), professor of Jewish ethics and mysticism at the JTS, the Orthodox Joseph D. Soloveitchik (1903–), and Reform's Eugene B. Borowitz (1924–) and Emil L. Fackenheim (1916–), spread beyond professional circles.

Conservative Judaism continued to grow the most quickly, appealing as it did to the American-born descendants of the Russian immigrants, who retained sentimental attachments to traditional practice. The movement numbered 217 congregations in 1948, 832 congregations in 1970. In 1971, 40 percent of a national sample described themselves as Conservative, 30 percent as Reform, and 10 percent as Orthodox. Reform congregations increased from 360 in 1948 to 698 in 1970. Some Orthodox synagogues became Conservative, and some Conservatives adopted Reform as a result of merger or the move to the suburbs.

Orthodoxy, the most authoritative branch in religious observance, was institutionally the most fragmented. In 1964 many of its approximately 1,600 synagogues were located in the older neighborhoods and had few members, and some were conventicles serving small groups or sects. The Orthodox community included a federation of modern congregations, most of whose rabbis were trained at Yeshiva College, which was reorganized as a university in 1945. The seven additional Orthodox seminaries indicate the continuing strength of European regional and sectarian forces in Orthodox circles. One of the signal achievements of Orthodoxy was its parochial-school system, which grew from 17 schools with an enrollment of 4,600 in 1935, to 400 schools with an enrollment of 85,000 in 1976.

The attitude of American Judaism to the growing demand of Jewish women for an equal place within the synagogue reflected the different religious outlooks and the influence of the feminist movement on Jewish life. Historically, Reform insisted on equal religious rights for women, at least in theory. In 1972, Hebrew Union College ordained the first woman rabbi. The Reconstructionist Rabbinical School accepted women from its founding in 1968. Conservative Judaism moved more slowly. In 1973, the association of Conservative congregations resolved that women be assured "equal opportunity to assume positions of leadership, authority and responsibility in all phases of congregational activity." However, the JTS resisted the mounting pressure to admit women to the course of study leading to ordination. These developments moved some Orthodox women to insist on upgrading religious education of girls and stimulated a debate in Orthodox journals and meetings on the place of women in Orthodox congregations. Meanwhile, in Jewish secular life a growing number of women assumed places of leadership as laypersons and professionals in the local federations and communal institutions as well as in national organizations.

At the extreme end of the Orthodox spectrum were the sectarian communities that arrived in the United States during and after World War II, bringing their segregated, Old World traditions with them. Aaron Kotler (1892–1962), a rabbinical leader and Talmudic scholar, established communities built around the higher study of the Talmud, "the heartbeat of Judaism," choosing the isolation of Lakewood, New Jersey, for his center. By the 1970s branches existed in dozens of cities. Hasidic communities established their

own self-contained neighborhoods. The larger Luba-
vitcher and Satmer sects, numbering an estimated
100,000, settled in sections of Crown Heights, Borough
Park, and Williamsburg in Brooklyn, New York. Several groups established village enclaves in Monroe and
New Square, New York.

The Sephardic Jews from the eastern Mediterranean
formed another subgroup of American Jewry. In the
wake of the Turkish revolt of 1908, the Balkan Wars of
1912–1913, and World War I, at least 25,000 emigrated
from the Balkans, Turkey, and Syria. They spoke
Judeo-Spanish (Ladino), Greek, or Arabic. Language,
religious culture, and ethnic background set them apart
from their Yiddish-speaking Ashkenazi neighbors. In
New York City, where 90 percent made their home, the
old Shearith Israel Synagogue took an interest in them,
but the Sephardim maintained their separate communal institutions on the Lower East Side and Harlem.
Differences among them in language and background
made coordinated activity difficult. Smaller synagogue
communities were established in Seattle, Los Angeles,
and Atlanta. Levantine Sephardim numbered an estimated 100,000 in 1970; they still maintain separate synagogues and, in the case of Brooklyn's Syrian Jews,
their own parochial schools. Although the third generation no longer speaks the ancestral languages, and
intermarriage with the Ashkenazim is high, they have
a great deal of ethnic pride. The descendants of one
small group of Jews from the island of Rhodes continue
to support synagogues separate from the other Sephardim in Seattle and Atlanta.

Secular societies and institutions were concerned with transmitting the cultural heritage as well. By the mid-1920s, six nonsectarian Hebrew teachers' colleges and a graduate school of Judaic studies, Dropsie College in Philadelphia, had been established. In addition to the Orthodox Yeshiva University, the Conservative JTS, and the Reform Hebrew Union College, American Jews established a nonsectarian liberal arts college in 1946, Brandeis University in Waltham, Massachusetts, which has a full curriculum in the arts and sciences and an important graduate program in Jewish studies. By the 1970s several hundred universities offered courses and majors in Jewish subjects. B'nai B'rith, essentially a fraternal order in its earliest years, turned to combating anti-Semitism and then broadened its interests to human rights. In the 1920s it established a network of Jewish campus centers, the Hillel Foundations, and a nationwide youth program. These and an adult-education program were the principal activities of the organization. Community centers also had extensive educational programs in the 1950s.

The Jewish press reflected this heightened interest in preserving group continuity. About 30 monthly and quarterly journals of opinion, scholarship, and belles-lettres were being published in the late 1970s. *Commentary*, published by the AJC, is widely read and considered one of the more influential periodicals in the nation. Fifty communities published weekly newspapers in the late 70s, but the shrinking number of Yiddish readers were left with only one daily, the *Forward*, and eight periodicals.

The great majority of Jewish Americans depended upon the religious school to assure Jewish continuity. Second- and third-generation parents maintained few traditions in the home, and the neighborhood and extended family no longer supplied an ethnic setting. The burden of Judaizing the young was assigned to the congregational school. Since this entailed the study of the Hebrew language, the task of the religious school was a formidable one. Reform temples offered Sunday schools, and the Conservative synagogues, afternoon schools two to four times weekly. Schoolmen decried the limited time that children attended religious school (three to five years for most). Some sent their children to all-day parochial schools (nearly all of them sponsored by the Orthodox); nearly everyone else found the system acceptable. In 1970, 84 percent of the young men (15 to 19 years) and 72 percent of the young women received some Jewish education. Most Jewish Americans clearly wanted their children to identify as Jews and be conversant in the essentials of their tradition but preferred a way that would not hamper their integration in American society.

The struggle to survive as a communal entity and still achieve integration often involved the question of marriage to non-Jews. The dichotomy between Christian and Jewish society in pre-Enlightenment Europe and the prejudice that continued after it generally precluded close relations between Jew and Gentile. In those cases of marriage between Jew and Gentile, it was the Jew who converted. There was no secular society, and conversion to Judaism was not feasible. As a result, Jews associated intermarriage with apostasy, and parents severed their ties with the defecting child.

Colonial Jewry and the German Jews responded to the open, pluralistic, and less stratified American society by intermarrying in increasing numbers. But the massive Russian immigration, concentrated in ethnic neighborhoods and having a stronger separatist tradition, remained far more endogamous. The intermarriage rate between Jews and Gentiles was only 1.17 percent in New York in 1908, and it remained at about 3 percent until 1940. In the following 20 years it hovered around 6.5 percent, then nearly tripled to 17.4 percent between 1961 and 1965. Of every 100 Jews who married in the years between 1966 and 1972, 32 married non-Jews. Approximately one-fourth of the intermarrying non-Jewish females converted to Judaism, but few non-Jewish males did so.

The sharp increase in intermarriage reflected wider social acceptance and changing attitudes. The proportion of Jews opposed to intermarriage declined from about 80 percent in 1965 to about 50 percent a decade later. A modern, nontraditional generation subscribing to the notion of marriage based on romantic love found it difficult to oppose intermarriage, especially when that could be interpreted as reverse discrimination. The attitudes of the intermarried themselves showed a blurring of once-distinct boundaries. Jewish spouses continued to identify themselves as Jews, and a significant number of non-Jewish wives identified themselves as belonging to the Jewish community. In the 1960s and 1970s, especially in the academic world, tolerance, belief in universal values, emphasis on individual fulfillment, and the weakening of religious and family ties created a fluidity in relationships among individuals and groups, which, however desirable, deepened the dilemma of the survivalists.

Jewish Americans are profoundly affected by their ties to world Jewry. The mass murder of European Jewry, the plight of hundreds of thousands of survivors, only a small part of whom were able to find refuge in the free world, and the dramatic struggle of the Jews of Palestine to achieve independence and absorb the refugees have produced an outpouring of support. American Jews placed the creation and survival of the Jewish state at the center of their concerns. Except for small groups on the extremes of the religious spectrum, notably the American Council for Judaism, established in 1943, all the religious denominations, service organizations, and secular movements joined to extend aid to Israel.

The support of American Jewry was critical. Under the leadership of Rabbi Abba Hillel Silver (1893–1963), American Zionists mobilized public opinion and political support in favor of establishing a Jewish state in Palestine. To get the United States to support the United Nation's resolution for the partition of Palestine into Jewish and Arab states (approved by the U.N. in November 1947), it was first necessary to convince President Harry S Truman to override the State Department's position that support for partition would permanently alienate the oil-rich Arab countries. On May 14, 1948, hours after Israel proclaimed its independence and the neighboring Arab states launched their attack on the fledgling state, Truman extended de facto recognition to Israel.

The continuing needs of the new state in resettling the remnant of European Jewry and Jews forced to leave the Muslim countries, together with the threat from its neighbors, made activity on Israel's behalf a permanent part of the American Jewish community structure. The ties to Israel drew upon deep sentiments. The beleaguered state was associated with the fresh memory of the Nazi holocaust—American Jews had failed to come to the aid of their helpless brethren in Europe; they now had the opportunity to extend assistance to the embattled Jews of Israel, the "saving remnant." The themes of guilt and atonement and of martyrdom and redemption pervaded theological literature and public discourse.

The relationship was reciprocal. The remarkable activization of the Jewish community at moments of supreme crisis, as in 1948 when the state of Israel was proclaimed and in the 1967 and 1973 wars, when its destruction appeared possible, reflected the importance of its well-being for the self-esteem of American Jews and as an essential element in their group identity. Support of Israel served as a secular-ethnic replacement for, or reinforcement of, religion. As the center of Hebrew culture, Israel enriched American Jewry. To the religious, its scholars, Talmudic academies, and holy places were the living links with the Diaspora, as they had been for millennia.

The continual appeals for aid to Israel generated

structural changes in the American Jewish community. Rising demands for overseas aid had encouraged the consolidation of fund-raising efforts in the 1930s; the dire situation in Europe and Israel in the 1940s and 1950s accelerated the trend. By the 1970s federations of Jewish philanthropies in 227 communities directed the raising and allocation of funds for local, national, and overseas needs. They also played an increasingly important role in organizing and planning local services such as family welfare, recreation, community relations, and care of the aged. About 60 percent of their funds was allocated to overseas needs, which after 1948 meant philanthropic and rehabilitation projects in Israel. About $6.9 billion was raised by the central Jewish community organizations between 1939 and 1976. The largest sum raised in a given year was nearly $600 million after the 1973 war; 82 percent of it was allocated to Israel. The Council of Jewish Federations and Welfare Funds, established in 1932, grew in influence as the local federations expanded. In 1955 the Conference of Presidents of Major American Jewish Organizations was formed as a consultative umbrella organization to deal with problems in the Middle East. Though these developments encouraged collaboration, only under the impact of the crises overseas did American Jewry achieve a modicum of organizational coherence. Even then, perhaps a third of the Jewish population remained outside the organized community.

New immigration underscored the complexity of the ties between Jewish Americans and world Jewry. The political and financial resources of the community were mobilized to help Jews who wished to leave the U.S.S.R. and others who were harassed for attempting to maintain their Jewish identity. But immigrants from Israel were often received with ambivalence and given no communal attention.

Spearheading the efforts on behalf of Russian Jews was the American Conference on Soviet Jewry. In addition to publicizing Soviet treatment of Jews, it and other Jewish organizations lobbied the U.S. government to intervene on the grounds that the Soviet government was violating human-rights agreements. The Jackson-Vanik Agreement, passed in 1973, linked the granting of most-favored-nation status to the U.S.S.R. to their adoption of a more liberal emigration policy. Between 1966 and 1977 about 130,000 Jews emigrated from Russia; some 15,000 of them came to the United States, and nearly half settled in New York City. Many were professionals and white-collar workers who had to accept lower-status employment; all found the transition to the free-market conditions of the United States difficult. Jewish organizations offered temporary financial support, aided the new immigrants in accommodating to American society, and integrated them into the Jewish community. Despite the experience of the organizations and an abundance of good will, the transition has often been distressing and difficult for the immigrants.

Since the founding of the Israeli state, as many as 300,000 Jews have emigrated from it to America. About half have settled in New York and another large contingent in the Los Angeles area. Some were Europeans or

Levantines who lived in Israel only briefly and found adjustment to its austerities too difficult. Others were long-time residents who saw greater opportunities across the ocean. Still others left because of the wars, near-wars, and threats of more wars.

The Israeli immigrants pose a problem for the Jewish community: they have chosen to leave the land that every Jewish American has learned to regard as a haven, the guardian of Jewish survival, and the center of Hebraic culture. The ambiguity toward the *yordim* ("those who descend," the Hebrew term for these emigrants, which has connotations of abandoning the land of Israel) has expressed itself in the absence of formal recognition of the Israelis as a Jewish immigrant group. Individuals have successfully established themselves in the professional and cultural life of the greater society and have contributed to the Jewish community as teachers and communal functionaries. Among themselves, the Israelis have almost no formal organization, though they have a lively informal social life. Many maintain close ties with the homeland, visit frequently, and in time of dire need have occasionally returned to fight in its defense.

Historical experience and religious culture fitted Jews for life in America. The intellectual discipline fostered by the Jewish religion, the social discipline required by life among hostile peoples, and urban mercantile skills facilitated their adaptation. Jews sought economic security in occupations with which they were familiar and which were least vulnerable to prejudice. Jews placed great store on deferring present rewards for future gains, and valued intellectual pursuit. In the 1970s the third and fourth generations of the great mass migration were a well-integrated body of citizens who accepted the values and mores of the United States and entered the public life of the nation with great vitality and few inhibitions. To that life they brought individual talents and a collective sensitivity toward the less fortunate.

Jews were no less well equipped for the task of maintaining their community. Their religious heritage and minority-group experience had provided them with the skills and social traditions to achieve this end. Survival preoccupied them, a preoccupation heightened by the holocaust and the establishment of the State of Israel. By the 1970s Jewish Americans could take pride in the flourishing communal life that had evolved in response to freedom and equality: a multiplicity of religious outlooks, successful absorption of diverse subgroups, a choice of ways to identify with the Jewish collectivity, and a comprehensive communal polity. Jews celebrated the Jewish-American experience as unique in the millenial history of the Diaspora; for a majority of those born Jewish, being at home in America had not lessened their will to survive as Jews. The interplay of the two realms—the Jewish and the American—had proven to be enriching, and Jewish thinkers declared such dual identity the essence of America's democratic pluralism.

Some survivalists sounded a dissenting note. Jewish life in America was only a pale reflection of the rich cultural and religious traditions from which it had sprung.

Moreover, the élan and the institutional strength of the community seemed to depend on external events, especially responses to the crises in Israel. These observers feared that when the peril passed, no other challenge would call forth a similar group commitment. A postwar generation which had neither experienced the social prejudices of their parents nor witnessed the holocaust, fully at ease in the United States, would drift away from ancestral moorings. If an increasing rate of intermarriage appeared to give credence to this view, Jewish life, now increasingly shaped by third and fourth generation Jewish Americans, also reflected vitality, adaptability, and the will to survive.

BIBLIOGRAPHY

Two broad-ranging surveys of the subject are Nathan Glazer, *American Judaism*, rev. ed. (Chicago, 1972), which stresses the religious and social aspects, and Henry Feingold, *Zion in America* (New York, 1974), the most recent and comprehensive study.

Jacob R. Marcus, *The Colonial American Jew, 1492–1776*, 3 vols. (Detroit, 1970), is a thorough study of the subject. Social and religious trends during the 19th century are treated in: Moshe Davis, *The Emergence of Conservative Judaism*, 2nd ed. (Philadelphia, 1965), and Leon A. Jick, *The Americanization of the Synagogue* (Hanover, N.H., 1976). Marshall Sklare, *Conservative Judaism* (1955; reprint, New York, 1972), places religious change in the 20th century within a sociological framework of the acculturation of American Jews; Charles S. Liebman, *Aspects of Religious Behavior of American Jews* (New York, 1974), includes important essays on the American rabbinate, Orthodoxy, and the Reconstructionist movement.

Irving Howe, *World of Our Fathers* (Philadelphia, 1976), is a massive and felicitous account of East European Jewry, focusing on New York and the Yiddish radical tradition; Hutchins Hapgood, *The Spirit of the Ghetto* (1902; reprint, Cambridge, Mass., 1967), is an evocative contemporary portrait; Charles S. Bernheimer, ed., *The Russian Jew in the United States* (1905; reprint, New York, 1970), contains valuable essays dealing with New York, Philadelphia, and Chicago. Moses Rischin, *The Promised City: New York's Jews, 1870–1914* (Cambridge, Mass., 1962), is a thorough social and intellectual account of the eastern European Jewish settlement of New York. Will Herberg, "The Jewish Labor Movement in America," *American Jewish Yearbook* 53 (1952), is the best brief survey of the topic. Local, regional, and institutional histories provide valuable insights. Some representative studies are: Joseph Brandes, *Immigrants to Freedom: Jewish Communities in Rural New Jersey since 1882* (Philadelphia, 1971); Stuart E. Rosenberg, *The Jewish Community in Rochester, 1843–1925* (New York, 1954); Steven Hertzberg, *Strangers within the Gate City: The Jews of Atlanta, 1845–1915* (Philadelphia, 1979); Max Vorspan and Lloyd P. Gartner, *History of the Jews of Los Angeles* (San Marino, Calif., 1970); Naomi W. Cohen, *Not Free to Desist* (Philadelphia, 1972); Arthur A. Goren, *New York Jews and the Quest for Community* (New York, 1970); Melvin I. Urofsky, *American Zionism from Herzl to the Holocaust* (Garden City, N.Y., 1975). Henry L. Feingold, *The Politics of Rescue* (New Brunswick, N.J., 1970), discusses the refugee problem in the 1930s and 1940s.

Marshall Sklare, *America's Jews* (New York, 1971), is an important analysis and sociological profile; Sidney Goldstein and Calvin Goldscheider, *Jewish Americans* (Englewood Cliffs, N.J., 1968), treats generation change in the Jewish community of Providence, R.I., with special reference to intermarriage, culture, and religion. Solomon Poll, *The Hassidic Community of Williamsburg* (New York, 1962), is a socioeconomic analysis of an ultra-Orthodox group. The most comprehensive treatment of Jewish communal structure and its operation is Daniel Elazar, *Community and Polity* (Philadelphia, 1976). Marshall Sklare, ed., *The Jew in American Society* (New York, 1974), and David Sidorsky, ed., *The Future of the Jewish Community in America* (New York, 1973), are important collections dealing with contemporary American Jewish experience.

The *American Jewish Yearbook*, which has appeared annually since 1900, is the most complete record of American Jewish life. The *Encyclopedia Judaica* (New York, 1972) contains valuable entries. The *American Jewish Historical Quarterly, Judaism, Commentary,* and *Midstream* are among the important scholarly periodicals and journals of opinion. William W. Brickman, *The Jewish Community in America* (New York, 1977), is the most comprehensive annotated bibliographical guide of books, and Jacob R. Marcus, *An Index to Scientific Articles on American Jewish History* (Cincinnati, 1971), is a bibliography of scholarly articles.

The two most important depositories of archival material are the American Jewish Archives in Cincinnati, Ohio, and the American Jewish Historical Society in Waltham, Mass.